INEQUALITY

AND

DEMOCRACY

Books in the

FUNDAMENTAL AWARENESS

IN ECONOMICS AND POLITICS

series

Book One

LOSING SOCIAL INTELLECT

The core reason behind the troubles
in Free Market Economy and Democracy

Book Two

COMPETITION AND CHEATING

The malfunctioning of
Free Market Economy and Democracy

Fundamental Awareness
in Economics and Politics

BOOK THREE

INEQUALITY
AND
DEMOCRACY

The real drivers of Growth and Welfare,
and when Democracy fails in optimising
Inequality

SALIH REISOGLU

Book Three published in 2026

ISBN 979-8-9922272-2-2

Contents

INTRODUCTION

Free Market Economy and Democracy are the main pillars of the western social order.

The economic and political theories underlying these systems are based on some *major hidden assumptions*. They assume that societies have *adequate Social Intellect*, while in practise they do not. And they assume that *Fair Competition reigns*, while in practise cheating dominates.

Books One and Two of this series revealed why and how these two major hidden assumptions in the economic and political theory, namely the existence of Social Intellect and the non-existence of cheating, both of which are spectacularly wrong, cause the malfunctioning of the western social order.

Book Three continues from where the previous two books left off.

THE SCOPE OF THE DISCUSSION

Book Three focuses on two major interrelated topics: *maximisation of the welfare of the society*, and *the conditions under which Democracy fails to cure the troubles in the economic system*.

On the welfare of the society, Book Three starts with the analysis of what welfare really is and how it can be maximised by optimally balancing inequality and economic growth. Next comes the analysis of how inequality and growth can be optimised through rising Social Intellect and establishing Fair Competition - while in practise most societies fail on both fronts, unnecessarily creating too high inequality and too low economic growth, ruining their welfare. And the analyses of some other essential policies covering taxation-and-distribution, in particular some common social security approaches that are goodwilled but actually over-dosed to the point of making more harm than good for the society, and some well-hidden taxation approaches that are necessary but missing, will complete the picture.

On the failure of Democracy in handling the troubles in the economic system, first the dynamics of the checks-and-balances between Free Market Economy and Democracy are briefly analysed, and then the major mystery in the western social order -namely, why Democracy, a one-man-one-vote political system based on absolute equality in principle, fails to prevent the emergence of excessive inequality on the economic front in practise- is addressed.

Finally, Book Three ties ends with Books One and Two, and reveals the alternate paths ahead for each society.

NO SPECIFIC SOCIETY IS TARGETED, BUT ALL ARE COVERED

As in all the books in this series, although no countries are mentioned, the primary focus of the discussion will be on the economically advanced western societies. However, all the discussed issues, analyses and potential remedies mentioned in the books can be applied to any society that exercises a Free Market Economy and Democracy. The readers are kindly requested to adopt the analyses and the conclusions to their own societies.

THE STYLE OF THE BOOK

The *Fundamental Awareness in Economics and Politics* series combine economics and politics, and therefore belong to a rather niche category in social sciences. Still, the books are written in plain language rather than in a scientific jargon, so that a reader interested in economics and politics can easily follow the flow of the ideas.

Thanks to the free flow of information and the availability of a huge supply of it, and the new attention attracters growing exponentially in the digital media, most of us now have ultra short spans of attention. In line with this reality, the book will not repeat the already-known and well-understood, but only concentrate on the significant but neglected or misunderstood. To respect the time and to keep the attention of the reader, all arguments are made as sharp and as short as possible.

CHAPTER 1

FUNDAMENTALS OF FREE MARKET ECONOMY AND DEMOCRACY

1.1 Clarifying The Basic Concepts

A System Of Checks And Balances

In any society, the owners of capital would like to be able to utilise their capital to produce and sell goods and services, earn profits, and accumulate these profits for further investments or future consumption. And, in order to be able to do that, they need an environment of law where ownership rights are established.

Historically, once some sort of environment of law is established, and the game begins, some succeed to earn and accumulate more capital than others, through whatever means, and eventually become major owners of capital. It does not take long for them to realize that they became a minority within the society, and if they cooperate among themselves rather than compete with each other, they can further increase their wealth at the expense of both the unorganized labour and the unorganized consumer – namely at the expense of the rest of the society. Next they realize that they need to support an authority who will sustain the social order in which they can continue to keep their status and prosper even further – fuelling the inequality to their benefit as much as and as long as possible.

However, there is a certain limit of increasing inequality within a society, before the losing crowds of consumers and labour eventually realize that they should somehow organize, become politically active, and get themselves heard and respected by the authority, so that they will have a say in law-making and thus can get more out of the economy for themselves. These crowds, namely the majority of the society, discover the need to initiate and maximise competition among the owners of capital, both for the demand for labour and in the supply of consumption goods, in order to prevent a minority to accumulate unfair amounts of wealth at the labour's and the consumers' expense. Thus was born the idea of Democracy, which asserts that legitimacy of the governing authority stems from the choice and the support of the society, rather than that of any minority. And thus, a social order is established where everybody has a say on politics, and politics has the ultimate say on the economy.

Today, in the economically advanced western societies, the economic system is based on Free Market Economy and the political system is based on Democracy. From the perspective of economic growth, Free Market Economy is indispensable. However, if left to its own devices, Free Market Economy creates too much inequality and too much concentration of power, as discussed in Book Two of this series. Thus, the current western social order was so designed that, the economic system based on Free Market Economy is checked-and-balanced by a political system based on Democracy, in which everyone has one and only one vote, and thus is subject to absolute equality.

The simple check-and-balance logic behind this social order is that, if and when the Free Market Economy creates too much economic inequality for whatever reasons, at the benefit of a minority and at the expense of the majority, the majority will use its political power within Democracy and a more socially conscious government will come to power, to take the necessary precautions to cure for the excessive inequality.

It is possible that, the policies applied by the socially conscious government may go too far in time, creating a society that is much more equal but much less motivated to try hard to develop. If and when this occurs, the growth rate will decline (and may even fall to negative), economic hardship will arise and the society will become unhappy again. Then, politics will step in once again, and through a democratic voting, a more economically liberal government will take over, to apply policy changes that will recover the motivation to innovate and develop, resulting in higher growth rates. But liberal economic policies may also be pushed too far in time, and will cause too much of a rise in inequality again, and thus politics will have to step in again, ... and the system will continue to oscillate between these alternate policies.

The value of these oscillations is that, by enabling a change in economic policies whenever required, they prevent the build up of social tension within the society and preserve the social order.

If and when these check-and-balance dynamics fail to function, for whatever reason, the society starts to lose faith in the whole system and social tension starts to build up. And in case such a build up continues untreated for long enough, the social order of the society may eventually break down: Democracy can practically be destroyed through shifting towards autocracy, Free Market Economy can be destroyed through excessive state control or interventions over markets and economy, and to put the final nail on the coffin, the supremacy of law may weaken or disappear. The society and its social order will then fall all the way to complete chaos.

The coming chapters will analyse the dynamics of this check-and-balance system, how and why these dynamics may fail to function as assumed, and what can be done to avoid the collapse of the western social order.

Economic Growth

The economic growth rate (shortly "growth rate" in the rest of the book) is assumed to be one of the easiest and best understood concepts in economics. But still, there is a devil in the details.

It is obvious that the overall wealth of a society increases as its economy grows, and the higher the growth rate the more will be the accumulation of wealth in the long run.

What is not so obvious, is how much wealth will be accumulated in the long run resulting from a certain rate of growth.

Growth rate is a variable mostly mentioned on an annual basis, and by nature it is mostly a single digit percentage. This enables the simplification of the relation of wealth accumulation versus growth rate in the short run, which, unfortunately, causes major misunderstandings for the case in the long run.

The trouble with the calculation of the effects of growth rates on the accumulation of wealth is that, growth rates do not add up, but get compounded by their nature. For the short run (say a couple years), the results of adding up and compounding come out to be pretty close, making many to believe that adding up is a good enough approximation. However, the results of adding up and compounding are totally different when the long run is considered.

To illustrate simply, assume that an economy has an annual growth rate of 4%. What will be its overall growth in 3 years? And in 30 years?

For the short run, namely 3 years, adding up gives the answer as 12% and compounding as 12.5%, thus adding up seems to be a good enough approximation.

For the long run, namely 30 years, however, adding up gives 120%, but compounding gives 224% - a tremendous difference[1]. Thus, any conclusions that are based on the wrong calculation (i.e. on the approximation) will be too far away from reality to be of any use in any analysis.

The significance of this observation for our analyses in the rest of this book is that, not only the growth rates, but also the *growth rate differentials between different economies* compound out to result in major differences in the overall wealth of the societies in the long run.

To illustrate, consider the economies of two different societies, both of which start at the same wealth level (say $100 billion) at Year 1, but one society experiences a constant growth rate of 2%, while the other experiences 4%.

Figure 1.1.A below shows the actual accumulated wealth for each society in the long term (the no-growth case, GR=0%, is also given as a reference).

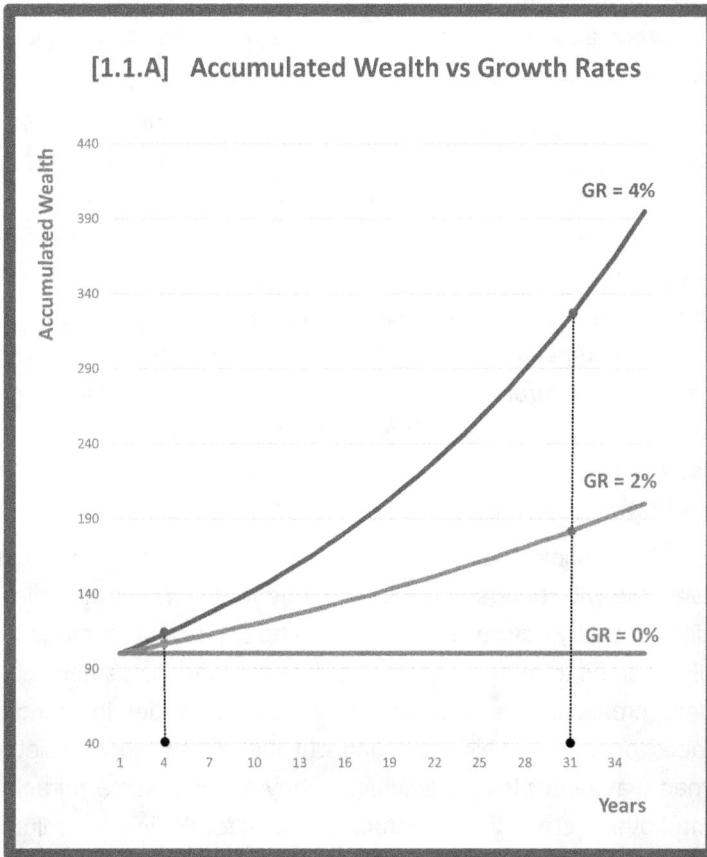

[1.1.A] Accumulated Wealth vs Growth Rates

As can be seen on the figure,

	Initial Wealth	Wealth after 3 years	Wealth after 30 years
GR = 2%	100	106.1	181.1
GR = 4%	100	112.5	324.3

This simple illustration reveals that, for the short run of 3 years (by the end of Year 4), the difference in the relative size of the two economies is around 6%, as can be expected through a simple approximation. However, for the long run of 30 years (by the end of Year 31), the difference in the relative size of the two economies is huge – and definitely way above the 60% guess one may make intuitively but mistakenly.

It is therefore important to keep in mind that, *small growth rate differentials between two economies in the short run compound out to result in huge differences in the overall wealth of these economies in the long run. What this means in practise is that, there is no need for miracles for one society to significantly surpass the other(s) in the long run. All that a society needs is a sustainable small difference in growth rates in the short run, accumulating through compounding to create a huge difference in its overall economic size (total wealth) in the long run. Realising this fact is crucial in understanding why the issues to be discussed in the coming chapters have a very significant effect on the wealth and welfare of the societies in the long run.*

In practise, societies mostly focus on how much a change in a certain policy variable will change in the growth rate in the short run (which is a small differential by nature, at best amounting to a few percentage points annually), but fail to realise the huge difference that such small changes eventually create in the long run. When they consider the long term differences once in a while, and find out that some other society has performed way better than themselves, they assume some miracle has happened over there in the meantime and look for finding that miracle to copy it. But in fact, there is no need for a miracle, and in most cases there isn't one anyway, but all that was needed (and achieved in cases of success) is a small but sustainable positive difference in the short term growth rates.

Income Inequality

Income inequality, namely the distribution of income within the society, is usually discussed within the framework of social justice. The coming sections and chapters will go beyond that, to analyse the not-well-recognized but significant effects of the changes in income inequality on the growth rate, wealth and welfare of the societies. In order to do so, first the definition of inequality has to be clarified.

The concept of *income per head* (a.k.a. "GNP per capita" in the economics jargon) is generally well known. In simple terms,

Income per Head = (total annual income of a society) / (total population),

thus, it just represents an *average* for the society.

Although it is widely used, this average income per head is an inadequate and misleading measure by itself unless it is accompanied by an indicator of income inequality. However, the measurement of income inequality is rather complicated and controversial. For that reason, in order to simplify the discussions throughout the book, conceptual levels of income inequality depicted in Figure 1.1.B will be used instead of other relevant indicators.

In the figure, the bottom of the inequality axis represents the theoretical absolute equality, namely the case where all the individuals in a society get the same share of income – in which case each individual's share is equal to the average income per head by definition.

The rest on the inequality axis are the practical cases. In all these cases, the total income of the society and the total population is kept constant. Therefore, *in all these cases, the income per head is constant. The only variable is the distribution of the total income* among the individuals making up the society.

Each case is represented by a sub-graph on the figure. In each sub-graph, the horizontal axis shows the different income levels, and the vertical axis shows the number of individuals at that particular income level. The dotted arrows show the spread between the lowest and the highest incomes that exists in that case. As the scales of both axes are kept constant at each sub-graph, the changes in inequality from case to case can be visualized easily without the need to read the actual values on either axis.

Moving up on the axis, first comes the case of low inequality, where the spread between the lowest and the highest incomes is rather small, and almost all individuals are close to the average income per head.

[1.1.B]   LEVELS OF INEQUALITY

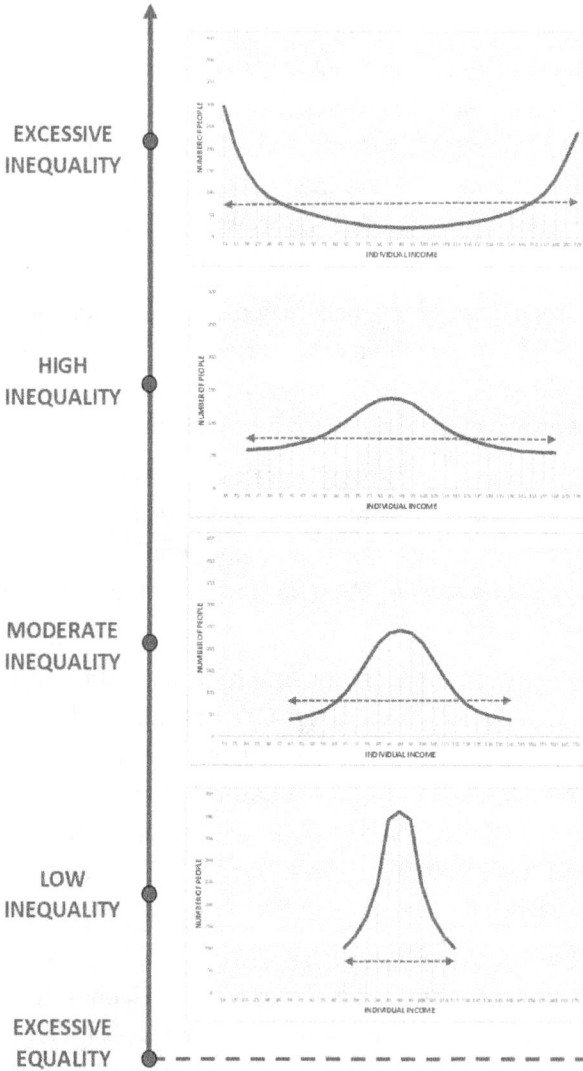

Next comes the case of moderate inequality, where the spread between the lowest and the highest incomes widens, and although the majority of the individuals are still close to the average income per head, there are also many individuals away from the average income per head, in both directions. This distribution, referred to as the bell-curve in the economics jargon, corresponds to a healthy income distribution from the viewpoint of growth and other economic variables, as will be discussed in detail later on.

Next case is high inequality, where the spread between the lowest and the highest incomes widens further, and there are more individuals away from the average income per head in both directions, than those close to the average income per head.

Finally comes the case of excessive inequality, where the spread between the lowest and the highest incomes are at its peak, and almost all individuals are away from the average income per head in both directions, with almost nobody at the vicinity of the average income per head. In the economics jargon, the so-called middle-class has disappeared. The catastrophic results of this case, in both the economics and politics fronts, will be discussed in detail later on.

Before moving further, it is important to observe that, *at the case of excessive inequality, the number of individuals at the lower extreme is practically much higher than the number of individuals at the higher extreme, due to the nature (i.e. the mathematical necessity) of rising inequality. This fact alone is supposed to strengthen the check-and-balance function of Democracy within the western social order, as Democracy is based on absolute equality among all individuals in terms of political representation. Thus, Democracy should easily annihilate excessive inequality, and actually push the economic system towards moderate inequality.* The reasons for its long lasting failure in practise will be analysed in the coming chapters.

1.2 The Relation Of Inequality And Growth Rate

Inequality and growth rate are the most significant variables determining the overall welfare of the society, as will be discussed in the following section. And to make life complicated, inequality and growth rate are not independent of each other. Their inter-dependence is critical but somewhat complex, thus its analysis requires the examination of several relevant dimensions of their relation.

DEMAND AND SUPPLY IN FREE MARKETS

In Free Market Economies, each product has a market, and each market consists of a supply and a demand side. On the supply side, to offer a product there is a need for capital (among other inputs), both for the initial investment and the production. On the demand side, for the consumption of a product there is a need for a customer base who both wants and can afford to buy the product. The demand for a product is maximized when the number of customers who want and can afford that product is maximised. The ability to afford a product, in turn, depends both on the total wealth of the society and the distribution of that wealth within the society.

In the discussion of inequality in the previous section, it was clear that the society can be thought to consist of three groups of individuals (i.e. customers): the low-income earners, the middle-income earners and the high-income earners. The distribution of the individuals in the society to these three groups determines the type of the inequality within the society: as shown by the figure by the end of the previous section, in societies with moderate inequality the middle-income earners dominate the society, while in societies with excessive inequality the middle-income earners are the minority, etc.

To facilitate the analysis, it helps to define and match the income levels with different types of consumption goods (or services): Low-income earners mostly consume inferior-goods, middle-income earners mostly consume regular-goods, and high-income earners mostly consume luxury-goods. If there is moderate inequality within a society, the income distribution curve is bell-shaped and the major consumption is made of regular-goods. As inequality rises, middle-income earners will be replaced by low and high income earners, and consequently, demand for regular-goods will be replaced by the demand for luxury-goods and inferior-goods. For the discussion of the growth rate, what matters is whether and how much the luxury and inferior goods can replace the regular-goods.

To simplify the analysis, assume that the changes in inequality do not cause any political and/or behavioural reaction in the society. This extremely unrealistic assumption will be removed later in this section, but for now it will enable the analysis of the dynamics of supply and demand as inequality changes.

To simplify further, consider a society with a closed economy (where there is no free flow of goods or capital to/from other societies), with free competition (with only marginal regulation) and with moderate income inequality (thus most individuals are middle-income earners, consuming regular-goods) to start with. Furthermore, assume that the individuals have no accumulated wealth and the social security system is weak, thus nothing can compensate the individuals for any changes in income.

As analysed in detail in Book Two of this series, when free markets are left to their own devices without any significant regulation[2] to provide and protect Fair Competition, the winners and the losers of the initial stages will soon turn to heavy-winners and heavy-losers, increasing income inequality at an ever-rising speed towards excessive inequality. The critical question in this section is what will happen to the growth rate as inequality will inevitably rise as time goes by.

To see the answer, the losing and the winning sides of the rising inequality have to be analysed separately.

Start with the losing side, namely with the individuals who lose their middle-income earner status and fall to low-income earner status. They will first lose the necessary income to consume their desired regular-goods. To escape a loss of consumption, they will initially borrow and continue to consume regular goods. However, sooner or later, they will reach the point where they can not borrow any further, but can barely pay the interest on their previous borrowing. Then they will have no choice but to start to consume inferior-goods. Eventually, a major share of their income will have to be allocated to paying interest, and they will start to fail to consume even the necessary inferior-goods – becoming victims of excessive inequality. And what happens then is not difficult to guess: the initial assumption of this section, namely *the changes in inequality not causing any political and/or behavioural reaction*, will be heavily challenged.

Before proceeding further, the developments at the winning side, namely with the individuals who leave their middle-income earner status and rise to high-income earner status, have to be considered. Initially, they will save some of their income (which will mostly be financing the borrowing of the losing side[3]), and also start to consume some more regular-goods and some luxury-goods. Remember that, the fall of consumption of regular-goods on the losing side is marginal initially, as they can borrow and continue to consume. Together with the rise of the consumption from the winning side, the total demand for regular-goods may then rise, practically resulting in an increase in the growth rate. However, this will not last long. The losing side will soon hit the limits of borrowing, coupled with continued loss of income, and thus will have to significantly decrease its demand for regular-goods. This fall in demand for regular-goods will not be offset by the winning side, as the falling marginal utility of any product will limit the consumption of regular-goods by those on the winning side. Instead, the winning side will start to demand more luxury-goods. As inequality rises further, and the losing side hits the limits of borrowing, the winning side hits the limits of lending. After that point, most of the savings of the winning side will have to go to some investments. In theory, these investments may then be channelled to the production of more luxury-goods, as well as more inferior-goods, as the demand for those two will be rising, replacing the demand for regular-goods. And therefore, in theory, if the increase in the production of the luxury and the inferior goods offsets the decrease in the production of the regular-goods, then the growth rate may continue to rise (or may stay the same) with rising inequality. In other words, growth rate and inequality may be independent of each other *in theory.*

POLITICAL REACTION IN DEMOCRACIES

To simplify the analysis of the relation of growth rate and inequality from the viewpoint of supply and demand, a practically irrational assumption - *that the changes in inequality do not cause any political and/or behavioural reaction in the society-* was deliberately made above. Under that unrealistic assumption, it came out to be theoretically possible that growth rate may continue to rise (or at least not fall) in spite of excessive inequality.

In practise, however, the rise in inequality towards excessive levels will result in some sort of political reaction sooner or later. As will be discussed in detail in the coming chapters, such a reaction will demand major changes in economic and social policies to decrease inequality towards moderate levels, usually coupled with a change in the governing party through a democratic election. Such a change in economic policies will eventually re-decrease the demand for luxury and inferior goods, and re-increase the demand for regular-goods, but in rather unpredictable ways and within unpredictable time frames, increasing the risks of all productive investments.

In practise, the silent build-up of a potential political reaction in the society, which in turn will demand and get a decrease in inequality, is easily anticipated by the investors on the winning side of the rising inequality, way before such a reaction surfaces on the political front. As a consequence, as inequality rises further in the short run, these investors may prefer to stay away from making productive-but-risky investments for the production of any type of goods, but rather channel their savings to unproductive-but-safer assets like real estate or precious metals. Then, the rising demand for luxury and inferior goods will not face an equivalent increase in supply, and thus will not result in an increase in production[4]. In other words, the decrease in the production of the regular-goods will not be offset by an increase in the production of the luxury and the inferior goods. In practise, therefore, *as inequality increases too much, the growth rate will decrease.*

FAIR COMPETITION, CHEATING, AND ALLOCATION OF RESOURCES

As discussed in detail in Books One and Two of this series, a society with adequate Social Intellect would establish Fair Competition, which in turn will optimise the allocation of the limited resources of the society and thus maximise the growth rate. If, however, the Social Intellect of the society is not adequate, or has weakened in time, then conditions of Fair Competition will be violated. The disappearance of fair opportunity in education and employment for the individuals will result in a fall in the quality of the human resources, which in turn will slow down innovation and technological development. The disappearance of Fair Competition among the competitors in the markets will enable cheating, and consequently, a rise of concentration of powers that will serve their own interests at the expense of those of the society. In short, the limited resources of the society will be terribly misallocated, which in turn will slow down the growth rate. In short, *weakening of Social Intellect decreases the growth rate.*

The loss of fair opportunity for the individuals, together with the rise of cheating and loss of Fair Competition in the markets, will also cause a rise in inequality way beyond moderate levels within the society. In short, *weakening of Social Intellect increases inequality towards excessive levels.*

As will be explained in the coming chapters, a society with adequate Social Intellect will be able to contain inequality around moderate levels, through many means. Thus, *a rise in inequality towards excessive levels almost always shows the weakening of Social Intellect*, which in turn reveals the loss of Fair Competition, *which in turn decreases the growth rate*. Reading all together, the weakening of Social Intellect and the consequent loss of Fair Competition, are the common factors behind the rise in inequality towards excessive levels and the slowdown of the growth rate. For that reason, *a rise in inequality towards excessive levels will be accompanied by a fall in the economic growth rate in practise.*

HUMAN BEHAVIOUR AND MOTIVATION, INNOVATION, PRODUCTIVITY

When Fair Competition and fair opportunity dominate the social order of the society, and consequently, when success is primarily based on merit, individuals will be motivated to develop themselves, work hard and perform their best, in order to improve their financial position and social status in the society. This motivation will in turn result in higher productivity and more innovation in the economy. Thus, the growth rate will rise both in theory and in practise.

However, if what an individual contributes to the society and what he gets in return is not fairly balanced, such that what the individual gets is much less than what he contributes, he will lose his motivation and will not bother to develop himself or work hard to maximise the value he creates for the society. In other words, *when an individual can not increase what he gets, he will decrease what he contributes to attain a fairer balance*. When such imbalances spread throughout the society, and most individuals start to behave that way, both productivity and innovation will fall in the economy, *eventually decreasing the growth rate*.

As the discussion above reveals, the primary condition for such imbalances to come out, is the lack of Fair Competition. As discussed in Book Two of this series, when there is Fair Competition, inequality can neither rise too high nor fall too low, but rather stabilise around moderate levels. Therefore, whenever there is too high or too low inequality, there must be a shortage of Fair Competition.

All the previous discussion in this section focused on the rise of inequality towards excessive levels. Indeed, when inequality rises too much for lack of Fair Competition, individuals on the heavily-losing-side will sooner or later realise that they do not have much a chance to improve their position whatever they do, and consequently lose their motivation. As, by the nature of excessive inequality, there are very many heavy-losers in the society, this will eventually result in a fall in productivity and innovation, and decrease the growth rate.

However, a case of loss of motivation also arises when there is too little inequality. As Fair Competition results in some moderate level of inequality, any economic policy that decreases inequality too much must hurt Fair Competition. In practise, this happens through either decreasing free competition too much or increasing taxation-and-distribution too much. In both cases, no one may lose against each other, but no one will win either. Therefore, the individuals with merit will not get what they deserve even if their contribution to the society is much higher than the rest. This time, these potential winners of a Fair Competition (if there were one) will lose their motivation, and the consequent fall in productivity and innovation will again result in a decrease in the growth rate. Moreover, too much taxation-and-distribution will result in another sort of terrible misallocation of resources, which also decreases the growth rate. In practise, therefore, *when inequality decreases too much, the growth rate will decrease.* As will be discussed in the next chapter, such a low growth rate will eventually cause a political reaction and a demand for an economic policy change.

CONCLUSION AND A CRITICAL OBSERVATION

For all the reasons analysed in this section, *when inequality rises or falls too much, the growth rate falls.* Therefore, *maximum growth rate is achieved at moderate inequality levels.*

In all the analyses above, the change in inequality is taken to be from a medium level towards too-high or too-low levels, and the conclusions are that, in both cases, the growth rates fall.

The rationale behind these analyses also works backwards. For instance, when a political reaction stemming from too high inequality eventually results in a policy change, establishment of a fairer competitive environment will both re-motivate individuals to perform better (thus, increasing productivity and innovation) and re-allocate resources in a better way, and consequently increase the growth rate. Or, when a political reaction stemming from a too low growth rate eventually results in a policy change, establishment of a fairer competitive environment which will introduce more inequality will re-motivate individuals to perform better (thus, increasing productivity and innovation), and a decrease in taxation-and-distribution will re-allocate resources in a better way, and consequently increase the growth rate. In both of these cases, *the changes in inequality towards medium levels rise the growth rates.*

The relation of inequality and growth rate revealed in this section is depicted in Figure 1.2.A.

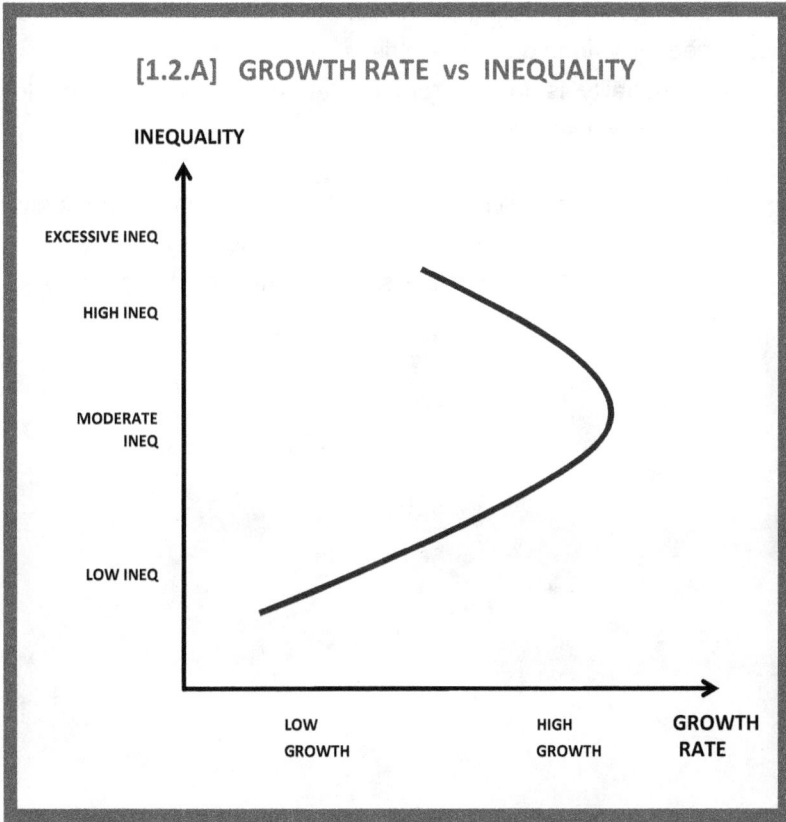

[1.2.A] GROWTH RATE vs INEQUALITY

It is important to emphasize that *the sole direction of change (a rise or a fall) in inequality is inconclusive on growth rate*[5]. *What matters is whether inequality is moving away from moderate inequality, in which case growth rate falls in both directions, or moving towards moderate inequality, in which case growth rate rises in both directions.*

To be more precise,

- if inequality is rising from low-inequality towards moderate-inequality, then growth rate rises,
- if inequality is rising from moderate-inequality towards high-inequality, then growth rate falls,
- if inequality is falling from high-inequality towards moderate-inequality, then growth rate rises,
- if inequality is falling from moderate-inequality towards low-inequality, then growth rate falls.

This critical observation will be utilised in the next chapter in the analysis of the dynamics of Free Market Economy and Democracy. Before moving on, however, the concept of welfare should be defined and clarified.

1.3   Welfare : A New Definition

Welfare From An Individual's Perspective

The concept of welfare can be better defined when an individual's perspective is analysed first. To simplify the analysis, assume that the individuals in a society have no accumulated wealth, thus the welfare of an individual is determined by his income.

ABSOLUTE INCOME VERSUS RELATIVE INCOME

For the analysis of the welfare of an individual, it is necessary to differentiate between his absolute income and relative income. *Absolute income* refers to the amount of income he earns. *Relative income* refers to the size of an individual's income with respect to the average income in the society. To be more precise, relative income refers to the standing of an individual's income within the income distribution in the society.

The welfare of the individual depends on both his absolute income and his relative income. However, their significance for the individual compared to each other, and thus their dominance on the welfare of the individual, is a complicated issue. In cases where there is low inequality, and thus the income distribution is narrow, relative income will be much less important than absolute income. But in cases where inequality is high, and thus the income distribution is much wider, relative income may even be more important than absolute income.

To clarify the situation it will help to consider a few simple cases, where an individual is asked to make the best choice to maximise his welfare.

In the case of low inequality, if an individual is asked to choose between
- (a) having 50 units of income
- (b) having 60 units of income,

his answer will be trivial: (b).

But when moderate or higher inequality exists, the situation gets more complicated.

If an individual is asked to choose between
  (a) having 50 units of income where the average income of the society is 10 units
  (b) having 60 units of income where the average income of the society is 100 units,

then, most probably, the answer becomes (a), as the major advantage of choice (a) in terms of relative income dominates the comparably smaller advantage of choice (b) in terms of absolute income.

However, if an individual is asked to choose between
  (a) having 50 units of income where the average income of the society is 10 units
  (b) having 200 units of income where the average income of the society is 240 units,

then, most probably, the answer becomes (b), as the major advantage of choice (b) in terms of absolute income dominates the comparably smaller advantage of choice (a) in terms of relative income.

As illustrated by these simple cases, while trying to maximise their welfare, most individuals do not have a definite priority of choice between absolute income and relative income, as either can dominate the other depending on their advantages for the individual compared to each other. This observation is critical for the proper understanding of the concept of welfare.

TYING MICRO AND MACRO VARIABLES

The absolute income and relative income of an individual are micro concepts that are introduced in this section. In the previous sections, the focus was on income inequality and growth rate, which are macro concepts. For the analysis of welfare, the relation between these two groups has to be clarified first.

If income inequality within the society is taken to be constant (i.e. the income distribution pattern and the relative incomes of individuals are assumed to stay the same), the absolute incomes of individuals rise as long as the growth rate is positive, and the speed of the rise of absolute incomes increase as growth rate rises[6]. Therefore, under a constant income distribution, *the absolute income of each individual is positively correlated with the growth rate*. In simple terms, if the individuals' shares of the cake stay the same, then any increase in the size of the cake will simultaneously benefit all the individuals.

If income inequality changes, then the relation gets complicated. For simplicity assume that there is no growth (i.e. the growth rate is constant at zero), thus there is no change in the size of the cake. Under this assumption, both the absolute and the relative incomes of individuals will change as inequality changes[7]. In practise, if an individual is on the losing side of the inequality (i.e. his personal income is below the average income of the society) to start with, then most probably he will lose further from increasing inequality. But if an individual is on the winning side of the inequality (i.e. his personal income is above the average income of the society) to start with, then he will most probably win further from increasing inequality[8]. Therefore, a change in inequality, independent of the direction of the change (i.e. whether it is increasing or decreasing), will effect different individuals in opposite ways. In simple terms, if the size of the cake stays the same, but the individuals' shares of the cake change, then, some individuals will benefit while some others will be hurt by the change. The key takeaway is that, *when inequality changes, everybody can not simultaneously benefit from it.*

And to make the analysis more complicated, in practise, both income inequality and growth rate change simultaneously – in other words, both the shares in the cake and the size of the cake change simultaneously.

WELFARE OF THE INDIVIDUAL

At the beginning of this section, the micro concepts of absolute and relative income are introduced, and it was explained that from the viewpoint of the overall increase in the welfare of the individual, either can dominate the other depending on their particular levels. Afterwards, these micro concepts are tied to the macro concepts, namely inequality and growth rate.

To sum up, the welfare of an individual depends on (or, in technical jargon, is a function of) two micro variables, namely his absolute income and his relative income. These two micro variables, in turn, are dependent on two macro variables, namely inequality and growth rate.

When the growth rate is dominant and inequality is stable, the welfare of the individuals change together in the same direction with the growth rate. In simple terms, when the size of the cake changes significantly while the shares of the individuals change relatively less, then a growing size will improve every individual's welfare and a shrinking size will hurt every individual's welfare. However, when the change in inequality is dominant and growth rate is only marginal in any direction, then different individuals will experience opposite changes in their welfare. The critical question is how the overall welfare of the society changes in this second case.

And finally, when changes in both inequality and growth rate are significant simultaneously, the outcomes above will overlap to determine the final outcome for each individual and thus for the society.

The Welfare Of The Society

The welfare of a society is simply the sum of the individual welfare of its members. It directly follows that, the change in the welfare of a society is the sum of the changes in the individual welfare of its members. The trouble arises from the fact that, when inequality changes, the changes in the relative incomes of some individuals occur at the expense of some opposite changes in the relative incomes of some other individuals in the society, and thus, while the welfare of some are rising the welfare of some others are falling simultaneously.

THE DYNAMICS OF CHANGE IN INEQUALITY

For simplicity of analysis, assume that there is no economic growth (i.e. the growth rate is constant at zero), thus there is no change in the total income of the society. A change in inequality, namely a change in the distribution of income among the individuals, may occur in different ways.

To illustrate, assume that initially the society is made up of 30 people, 10 people having an income of $20, 10 people $40, and 10 people $80. Then a redistribution occurs (without any change in the total income of the society) such that inequality rises.

After one possible redistribution, if 3 people who used to earn $20 now earns $15 (decreasing their welfare) and 1 person who used to have $80 rises to $95 (increasing his welfare), the incomes of others remaining the same, the number of losers will be more than number of winners, thus intuitively, it is clear that the society's cumulative welfare falls[9].

However, after another possible distribution, if 1 person who used to earn $20 falls to $5 (decreasing his welfare) and 3 people who used to earn $80 rise to $85 (increasing their welfare), the incomes of others remaining the same, the number of winners will now be more than number of losers. Thus, by the same intuition used above, the society's cumulative welfare seems to rise, although inequality has increased in an environment where there is no growth. As this second case looks strange, something must be wrong in trying to analyse the change in the cumulative welfare of the society by solely comparing the numbers of individual winners and losers after the redistribution.

THE CONCEPT OF MARGINAL UTILITY

The catch in the second strange case above is that, an income of $1 has a much higher value for the person who earns $20 compared to those who earn $80. Because of this *marginal utility* of income, a unit change in income is *not* equivalent to the same amount of change in welfare at different income levels. For those with low income, a unit change in income brings a significant change in welfare, while for those with high income, a unit change in income brings just a slight change in welfare. Therefore, when the person who used to earn $20 falls to $5, his welfare is ruined. But when the 3 people who used to earn $80 rise to $85, their welfare has only marginally increased. Thus, in the second case above, although the number of winners is larger than the number of losers, as the amount of fall in the welfare of the losers is much larger than the total amount of rise in the welfare of the winners, the cumulative welfare of the society still decreases. And now, both cases of distribution discussed above give the same result in terms of the overall change in the welfare of the society: when there is not much of a change in the total income of the society, a rise in inequality will have a negative effect on the overall welfare of that society.

THE WELFARE OF THE SOCIETY

The analysis in this chapter revealed that *the welfare of the society eventually depends on two variables, namely the economic growth rate and the level of inequality within the society.* Or, in simple terms, the welfare of the society depends on both the size of the cake and the distribution of the cake among the individuals.

When either one of these variables are taken into consideration solely, keeping the other constant, two easy conclusions on the direction of change in the welfare of the society emerge: *welfare of the society rises as economic growth rate rises, and, welfare of the society falls as inequality rises.*

However, when both these variables are changing simultaneously, quantifying the change in the welfare of the society is far from trivial. This is due to the fact that, when significant changes occur in both variables simultaneously, a *unit change* in either of these variables will result in a different amount of change in welfare depending on the *values* of both of these variables[10]. Therefore, the rest of the analysis will just be based on a conceptual and visual description of the change in welfare against these two variables.

Starting with the extremes, when growth rate decreases too much, even though inequality may be moderate or low, its effect dominates welfare and decreases it significantly. Similarly, when inequality rises too much, even though the growth rate may still be positive, its effect dominates welfare and decreases it significantly. In between, namely when both variables are around their moderate levels, none of them dominate the other, and welfare is above the levels defined by the two extremes. Therefore, somewhere between the extremes, when neither growth rate is too low, nor inequality is too high, the welfare of the society reaches its maximum level.

Consequently, this relation of the welfare of the society versus the growth rate and the inequality within the society can be represented by the graph on Figure 1.3.A.

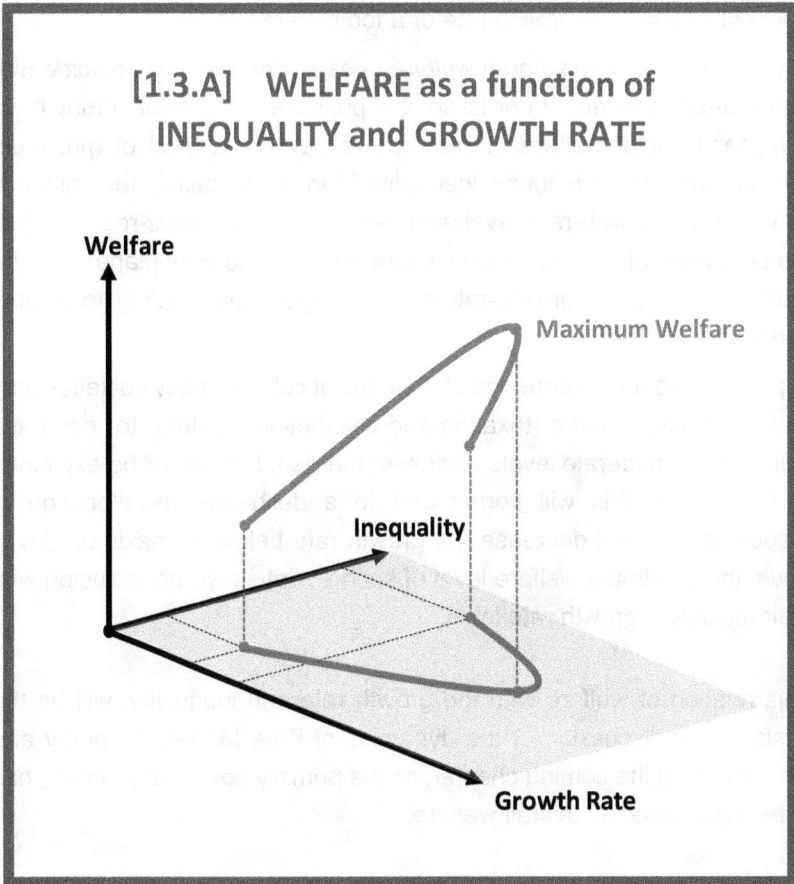

[1.3.A]   WELFARE as a function of INEQUALITY and GROWTH RATE

Welfare

Maximum Welfare

Inequality

Growth Rate

Notice that the relation of growth rate and inequality shown in Figure 1.2.A in the previous section, is the surface defined in light-grey in Figure 1.3.A above. The values of welfare that corresponds to each combination of inequality and growth rate on the grey surface are shown in the third vertical dimension. When inequality is too high, welfare falls to a minimum level. Similarly, when growth rate is too low, welfare falls to another minimum level. And between those two extremes on the inequality vs growth rate plane, welfare has higher levels, thus some maximum level somewhere in between.

To re-emphasize, this relation shows that, to maximise its overall welfare, a society needs to balance its growth rate and inequality, staying away from either a too low growth rate or a too high inequality.

Finally, notice that *maximum welfare does not necessarily coincide with maximum growth rate*. In practise, it is possible that a society may have a higher level of welfare at somewhere below the level of maximum growth rate but with lower inequality[11]. In such cases, the distance between the growth-rate-level-where-maximum-welfare-is-reached (i.e. the projection of the maximum welfare point on the grey plane) and the maximum-economic-growth-rate-level changes from society to society and from time to time.

In practise, as a consequence of their social culture, many societies may prefer to have some taxation-and-distribution system to decrease inequality to moderate levels whenever needed. But, as will be explained in Chapter 4, this will correspond to a deliberate misallocation of resources, and will decrease the growth rate below its maximum level. Thus, the maximum welfare level of such societies will not coincide with their maximum growth rate level.

This relation of welfare with the growth rate and inequality, will be the basis of our discussion of the dynamics of Free Market Economy and Democracy in the coming chapter, as the primary goal of any society has to be maximising its overall welfare.

CHAPTER 2

THE SEARCH FOR OPTIMAL POLICY

2.1 Economic Policies And Policy Cycles

Consider a society with enough Social Intellect to establish a social order based on some version of Free Market Economy and Democracy. Thus, it has a competitive economy, and a political control over the conditions of that competition through some laws and regulations, and it has some social security system that may include some taxation and distribution. It realizes that its welfare depends on both its income (and thus economic growth rate) and the distribution of that income (and thus inequality), and therefore it cares about both. However, it is not intellectual enough yet to determine the Optimal Policy that will balance growth rate and inequality in such a way that its welfare will be optimized.

In such a society, there are two fundamental economic policies in principle, namely *Liberal* and *Social*, with many variants in practise.

The society is learning by trial and error, through shifting between these liberal and social economic policies (variations of which may be represented by many political parties). Naturally, it does not tolerate either a too low growth rate or a too high inequality, and therefore, whenever one of these extremes are hit, it demands a policy change in order to cure that.

Liberal And Social Economic Policies

Liberal Policy primarily defends more freedom to win or lose, based on the principle that individuals must bear the consequences of their own choices. The significance of the potential difference between winning and losing (also referred to as *the carrot and the stick* in the economic jargon) is the driver of individual motivation to perform one's best, and such maximisation of performance of each individual in turn generates a cumulative higher growth rate for the society. In line with that principle, to keep the potential difference between winning and losing significant, the social security system should not be over-compensating, and in particular the taxation and redistribution of income (or wealth) should be marginal or non-existent. The concept of introducing more freedom to the economy includes the deregulation of the economy in every dimension as much as possible and the increase of the flexibility in the labour market.

Social Policy, on the contrary, defends more of a tilt towards economic equality, believing that not all the outcomes faced by an individual are consequences of his own choices, but may be due to other reasons such as luck or lack of fairness or even cheating. Therefore, the potential difference between winning and losing, if it reaches extreme levels, has to be corrected by the society. For that reason, a strong social security system, including higher taxation and redistribution -if and when required-, has to be established. Market regulation has to be strengthened to protect the interests of the consumers against the producers, the interests of the society against the market participants, and the interests of labour against the employers, and most importantly, to prevent the emergence of concentrations of economic power which decrease competition in the markets[12].

In simple terms, therefore, Liberal Policy focuses on growing the size of the cake, while Social Policy focuses on the distribution of the cake. Thus, both policies entail trade-offs between inequality and growth rate, but in opposite ways.

STAGES OF ECONOMIC POLICIES

Both of these economic policies have three stages:

- Initial Stage
- Maturity Stage
- Over-dose Stage

All the stages of both of these policies will be discussed in detail in the coming sub-sections, however, an initial overview will facilitate the coming discussion.

The *Initial Stage* is when the new policy is being implemented following a change from the previous policy. This stage generally succeeds in increasing the welfare of the society in the short run, as it is practically a reversal from the previous policy which have decreased the welfare of the society to minimum levels and created a positive base effect for the next policy.

Next comes the *Maturity Stage* of the policy, where it is completely implemented and its effects on growth rate and inequality are fully revealed. In general, the welfare of the society is *maximised in the short run* during this stage. (It is crucial to pre-emphasize that, maximising welfare in the short run is not the same as maximising welfare in the long run – as will be explained in the coming sections.)

And the *Over-dose Stage* of the policy is when the fundamental principles of the policy are pushed to the extremes, and thus the negative side effects dominate and decrease the welfare. As the Liberal Policy focuses on growing the size of the cake, when its principles are pushed to extremes, it faces trouble on the distribution front. Similarly, as the Social Policy focuses on the distribution of the cake, when its principles are pushed to extremes, it faces trouble on the growth rate front. For both policies, therefore, at the over-dose stage their harms start to outweigh their benefits, and the welfare of the society is minimised again, paving the way for a democratic demand for a policy change.

Policy Cycles

As each policy eventually reaches its over-dose stage and the welfare of the society hits minimum levels in the short run, a political demand arises for a change and the current policy is replaced by its alternative. This process creates a cycle of economic policies as depicted by Figure 2.1.A below.

[2.1.A]   POLICY SHIFTS AND CHANGES

LIBERAL POLICY		OVER-DOSE LIBERAL POLICY
* Initial Stage / rising Welfare	Slow gradual shift in policy	* Over-dose Stage / falling Welfare
* Maturity Stage / maximising Welfare		
Sustainable for a long period		Short lived

POLICY CHANGE   Alternative Policy Change   POLICY CHANGE

OVER-DOSE SOCIAL POLICY		SOCIAL POLICY
* Over-dose Stage / falling Welfare	Slow gradual shift in policy	* Initial Stage / rising Welfare
		* Maturity Stage / maximising Welfare
Short lived		Sustainable for a long period

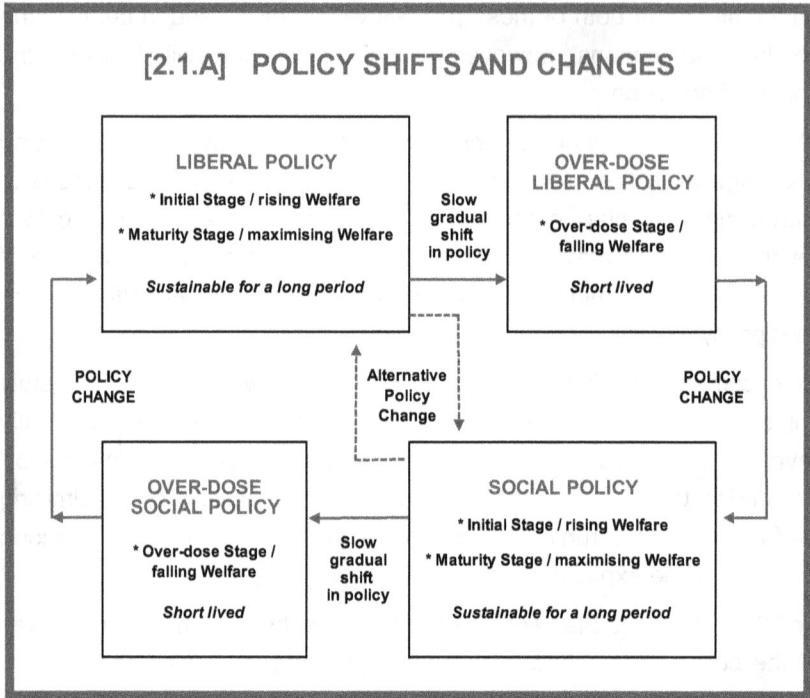

Before proceeding with the details of each policy, some common characteristics can be high-lightened.

The society may spend a long time during the moderate policy applications, namely during the initial and maturity phases, as welfare rises and eventually maximises in the short run. However, in many cases (especially where the Social Intellect of the society is inadequate), such success of a policy will ignite a further -though usually slow and gradual- shift towards the extremes. *Once extremes are reached, the over-dose stage is usually short lived* as the welfare of the society starts to decrease fast and falls to a minimum level in the short run, and a demand for a policy reversal emerges.

In general, *the time spent at each stage of each policy varies from society to society, and time to time within each society,* depending on the prevailing economic, political and social conditions, locally and globally.

The Dynamics Of Policy Cycles

In the coming sub-sections the changes in the growth rate, inequality and welfare will be analysed for each stage of each economic policy. While discussing these dynamics, assume that the society has a closed economy - there is no free trade and no flow of capital or labour in or out of the society. This will simplify the analysis, without changing the main conclusions.

During the analyses in the coming sub-sections, it will help to refer to Figure 2.1.B to visualize the flow from each stage of each policy to the next one.

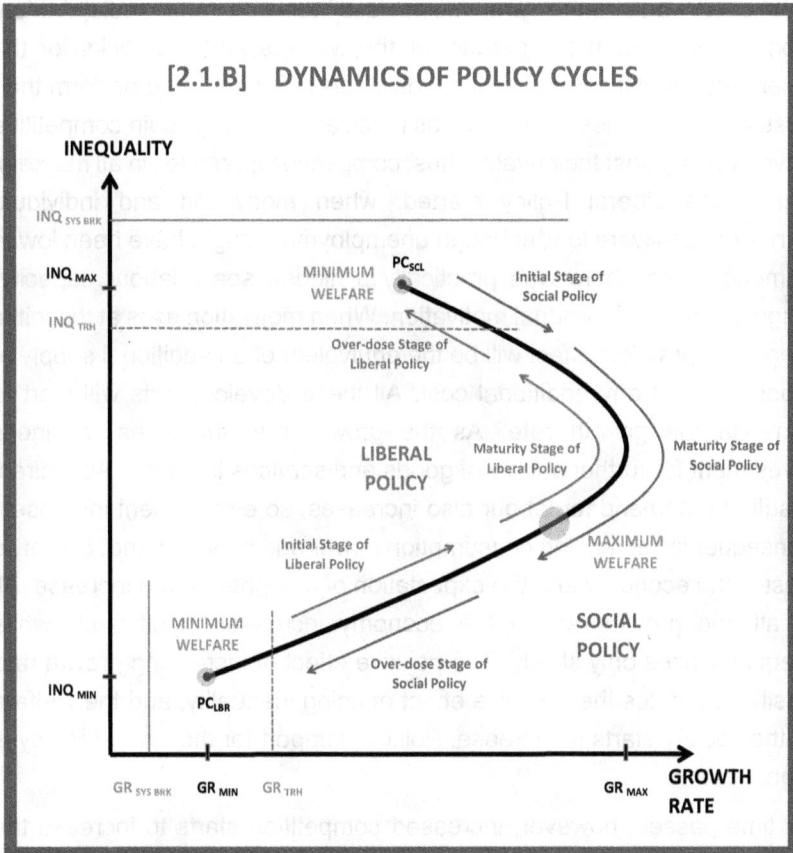

[2.1.B] DYNAMICS OF POLICY CYCLES

A Closer Look At Liberal Policy

Consider some point in time, when the society has a very low level of inequality (INQ_{MIN}), but also a very low, or probably negative, growth rate (GR_{MIN}). As the negative effect of the very low growth rate dominates that of low inequality, the welfare of the society is at a short-term minimum. The society demands a new economic policy that will increase its welfare, and through a democratic process comes the beginning of the Liberal Policy (PC_{LBR}).

At the initial stage of the Liberal Policy, deregulation starts in the economy, including a rise in the flexibility in the labour market, practically resulting in a decrease in labour rights. The social security system is weakened, and there are much less taxation and redistribution. Consequently, both the carrots for the winners and the sticks for the losers are magnified, motivating individuals to try harder to perform their best, and companies to innovate as much as possible to gain competitive advantage against their rivals. Thus, competition increases in all markets. Before the Liberal Policy started, when motivation and individual performances were low, although unemployment might have been low in numeric terms, there was practically a hidden spare labour capacity, disguised as low individual motivation. When motivation rises at the initial stage, the practical effect will be the equivalent of an additional supply of labour without any additional cost. All these developments will start to increase the growth rate. As the growth rate increases, business investment for further supply of goods and services increase. As a direct result, the demand for labour also increases, so employment increases, consequently increasing consumption power and thus demand. Society's trust in the economy and the expectation of a brighter future increase. All in all, the growth rate of the economy increases significantly while inequality rises only slowly. The positive effect of increasing growth rate easily dominates the negative effect of rising inequality, and the welfare of the society starts to increase. Political support for the Liberal Policy is high.

As time passes, however, increased competition starts to increase the income gap between winners and losers. On the one hand, individual merits, successful investments, or mere good luck, start to provide higher rewards to winners. On the other hand, unsuccessful risk taking, individual weaknesses in merit, or mere bad luck, start to create heavy losers. And there is no strong social security system left to make up for the difference. Although the growth rate continues to increase, its rate of increase is slower than that at the very beginning. Inequality, however, starts to increase at a faster rate. Although welfare is still rising, its rate of rise is slowing down.

After some time into the mature stage of the Liberal Policy, the negative effect of the increase in inequality balances out the positive effect of the increase in the growth rate, and the welfare of the society reaches its short-term maximum, starting to fall afterwards, albeit slowly. Afterwards, the rate of increase in the growth rate further slows, and eventually the growth rate peaks (GR_{MAX}). From that point on, as inequality increases further, the growth rate starts to decrease, and consequently, welfare starts to fall faster.

As the liberal policies are pursued further in the over-dose stage of the Liberal Policy, trouble starts to build up. The winners in the markets will re-compete among themselves and create a new smaller set of winners each time, as the set of losers expand. Due to lax regulation, sooner or later cheating spreads in the economy, and concentrations of power (including monopolies and oligopolies) start to dominate many markets. Consequently, as discussed in detail in Book Two of this series, competition starts to decrease in these markets, at the expense of the consumers and the labour. This in turn, further increases competition in some other markets. The economy reaches a point where some markets are under-competitive and others are over-competitive, none functioning properly. In all cases, labour starts to get less of a share from the cake, and inequality continues to rise ever faster. As growth rate is also decreasing, the welfare of the society starts to decrease at a faster pace, pulling down the political support for the Liberal Policy.

Eventually, inequality will approach to excessive levels, and pass above some *high inequality threshold* level (INQ_{TRH}), such that the society loses its faith in the Liberal Policy, reacts politically and demands a policy change to some Social Policy[13].

In a Democracy, a policy change usually comes with an election where another political party comes to power, following the demand for a change from the Liberal Policy to a Social Policy.

The inherent problem here is that, the pre-determined time of the next election may not be soon enough. During the time between the emergence of the demand by the society for a policy change and the time of the election -thus the actual policy change-, inequality continues to increase, the growth rate continues to decrease, and consequently the welfare of the society falls further.

The danger here is that, if the inequality increases too much in the meantime, and passes beyond some *inequality system breakdown* level (INQ_{SYSBRK}), such that the society loses all its faith in the existing system of Free Market Economy and Democracy, beyond losing faith in the existing policy, then, the reaction of the society will become unforecastable and the whole social order of the society will be in danger of breaking down irreversibly[14].

To clarify, at *high inequality threshold* level (INQ_{TRH}), the society loses faith in the current policy and/or politicians on duty, and demands just a policy change. The alternative policy is ready and known. As long as the change of policy and the politicians on duty is made without much delay, the functioning of the overall economic and political systems (i.e. the social order) remains intact. But if the *inequality system breakdown* level (INQ_{SYSBRK}) is reached, because of some intentional or unintentional delay, the society will lose its faith in the overall economic and political systems, and thus the social order may collapse, this time without knowing what may come next. Therefore, it is for the best interest of the society and all of its members, including the politicians on duty, to call for early elections whenever a political demand for a policy change arises in the society but the scheduled election date is too far in the future.

Needless to say, both the high inequality threshold and the inequality system breakdown levels change from society to society, and from time to time for each society. Therefore, it would be a dangerous practise to try to guess where they may be and test the limits, as once the answer clarifies it may be too late to save the social order.

A Closer Look At Social Policy

When the change from Liberal Policy to Social Policy eventually occurs (PC_{SCL}), the welfare of the society has fallen to a minimum level, with very high inequality (INQ_{MAX}) and a low growth rate.

At the initial stage of the Social Policy, social spending, financed through higher taxes, is increased to transfer income from the previous winners to the losers, and inequality starts to decrease fast. This redistribution of income increases both the current and potential consumption of the society, increasing demand. There would probably be a spare capacity on the supply side, as the demand had fallen fast at the over-dose stage of the previous Liberal Policy, and thus supply can immediately respond to the increased demand, and in turn increase the growth rate. The potential increase in consumption may reignite investments, conveniently financed by the already accumulated savings in the previous stage, and in turn investment spending increases, which in turn increases demand for labour. Simultaneously, regulations are strengthened to minimise cheating, and to protect the interests of the consumers against the producers and the interests of labour against the employers. Most importantly, anti-trust laws are enacted and enforced to eliminate the concentrated economic powers and reinstall competition in under-competitive markets, which in turn rebalances competition in the overall economy. As growth rate is increasing fast while inequality is falling, welfare is also increasing fast. Political support for the Social Policy is high.

As time passes, however, increased social spending starts to weaken both the carrots for the winners and the sticks for the losers, demotivating individuals from trying harder to perform their best or to innovate. This loss of motivation practically starts a hidden decrease in the labour force, without a measured decrease in employment or the labour costs. The motivation to take significant business risks starts to weaken too, and all sorts of investments start to slow down. Although growth rate continues to increase, its rate of increase is slower than that at the beginning. Inequality continues to fall and thus welfare is still increasing.

After some time into the mature stage of the Social Policy, the rate of increase of the growth rate slows further down and eventually the growth rate reaches its peak (GR_{MAX}), and then starts to decrease. Inequality continues to fall, and welfare is still increasing, but now at a slowing pace. Towards the end of the mature stage, the negative effect of the decrease in growth rate eventually balances out the effect of the continuing decrease in inequality, and welfare of the society reaches its short-term maximum, starting to fall afterwards.

As the social policies are pursued further in the over-dose stage, pushing regulations too far, while strengthening social security too much, trouble starts to build up. When too little inequality is left with too much security, people lose their motivation to compete hard and to innovate. When too heavy taxation and over stretched regulation enter the picture, businesses lose their motivation to take risks and make investments. And this time the problem emerges on the supply side. Consequently, the growth rate starts to fall at a faster pace, and may even turn to negative, while, to worsen the situation, inequality starts to fall at a slower pace. Thus, the negative effect of the change in growth rate dominates, and welfare starts to fall ever faster, pulling down the political support for the Social Policy.

Eventually, the decrease in the growth rate falls below some *low growth rate threshold* level (GR_{TRH}), such that the society loses its faith in the Social Policy, reacts politically and demands a policy change to some Liberal Policy.

Once again, in a Democracy, a policy change should come with a timely election, because of the fact that, between the emergence of the demand by the society for a policy change and the time of the election -thus the actual policy change-, growth rate continues to decrease and dominate the welfare, consequently decreasing the welfare of the society further. The danger here is that, if the growth rate decreases too much in the meantime, and falls below some *growth rate system breakdown* level (GR_{SYSBRK}), such that the society loses all its faith in the existing system of Free Market Economy and Democracy, beyond losing faith in the existing policy, then, the reaction of the society will become unforecastable and the whole social order of the society will once again be in danger of breaking down irreversibly.

To clarify, at *low growth rate threshold* level (GR_{TRH}), the society loses faith in the current policy and demands just a policy change, and as long as the change of policy is made without much delay, the functioning of the overall economic and political systems (i.e. the social order) remains intact. But if the growth rate system breakdown level (GR_{SYSBRK}) is reached, because of some intentional or unintentional delay, the society will lose its faith in the overall economic and political systems, and thus the social order may collapse. Once again, it is for the best interest of the society and the politicians on duty, to call for timely elections whenever a political demand for a policy change arises in the society.

Needless to say, both the low growth rate threshold and the growth rate system breakdown levels change from society to society, and from time to time for each society. Again, it would be a dangerous practise to try to guess where they may be and test the limits, as once the answer clarifies it may be too late to save the social order.

When the change from Social Policy to Liberal Policy eventually occurs (PC_{LBR}), the welfare of the society has fallen to a minimum level, with very low growth rate (GR_{MIN})[15] and very low inequality (INQ_{MIN}).

And then, the cycle re-starts.

And as long as the Social Intellect of the society shows no significant improvement, this cycle will repeat again and again.

A Final Observation On Policy Cycles

Notice that both the liberal and the social policies have common characteristics regarding their flow through their stages.

At their initial stages, growth rate rises, inequality moves from extremes towards moderate levels, and consequently welfare increases.

At their maturity stages, growth rate is maximised, inequality is around moderate levels, and consequently welfare is maximised in the short run.

At their over-dose stages, inequality moves away from moderate levels towards extremes, growth rate falls, and consequently welfare decreases.

The crucial observation to be made here is that, *if the over-dose stages of both polices can be shortened, then by the completion of a full liberal plus Social Policy cycle,*

- the average growth rate throughout the cycle will be higher, thus the long-term economic growth will be higher,
- the range of inequality throughout the cycle will narrow around moderate levels,

and consequently,

- *the average welfare throughout the cycle will be higher.*

Therefore, one critical question to be analysed in the next section is how this can be achieved.

2.2   Travelling On The Learning Curve

Social Intellect

Social Intellect, the primary determinant of how well the economic and political systems of a society work, was discussed in detail in Book One of this series. Still, a brief reminder of the basics that are most relevant to the ongoing analysis can be beneficial.

WHAT IS SOCIAL INTELLECT

Social Intellect is a balanced blend of intelligence, social education, social experience and social awareness.

Having adequate Social Intellect can be defined as having some basic education and accumulated experience in *social sciences* that improve an individual's *awareness of the social environment* around him, both as *a political participant* (at least as a voter) and as *an economic participant* (at least as a consumer and a supplier of labour) in the society.

Consequently, social education must span the basics of the primary social sciences of politics, economics, finance, law and sociology. In common practise, societies and individuals try their best to invest in education targeting professional expertise in many specific fields, and produce many experts who add value to the society, but unfortunately, *such professional education is not social education, and does not enable an individual to have adequate Social Intellect.*

Needless to say, the aim of social education is not, and can not be, to create an economics or politics expert out of each individual. All that is required of social education is to make each member of the society intellectual enough to be able to understand and evaluate the analysis of the real experts in social sciences, so that he can attain and keep social awareness, and make rational decisions as a consumer and a voter.

Finally, *social awareness* is the continuous process of spending time and effort to observe and understand the developments in economics and politics both within the society and globally.

SOCIAL INTELLECT IS A RELATIVE CONCEPT

The Social Intellect and awareness of the individual should enable him to make rational decisions regarding economic and political issues. Making rational decisions, in turn, requires understanding causations, namely the chain of events from the reasons to the results. Consequently, the more complex the environment gets, the harder will be understanding causations in economic and political matters. It directly follows that a more complex environment necessitates a higher Social Intellect for rational decision making.

Therefore, *Social Intellect is a relative concept*, as it concerns *the intellectual level of the society compared to the complexity of the economic and political environment in which it needs to survive.*

THE PRACTISE VERSUS THE PRINCIPLE

Within the framework of Free Market Economy and Democracy, in principle, the individuals, and thus the society, are assumed to have adequate Social Intellect. However, in practise, a society's overall Social Intellect may be inadequate with respect to the complexity of the environment.

In this section, the analysis of the changes in policy cycles through time will start with a society that has inadequate Social Intellect with respect to the complexity of its environment, and examine what happens as the society develops its Social Intellect towards adequacy. The complexity of the environment is assumed to stay the same, so that the society can develop its Social Intellect through gaining further experience through each cycle, namely through trial and error. This unrealistic assumption will then be removed in the next section, and the consequences will be discussed.

Initial Effects Of Rising Social Intellect On The Policy Cycle

Starting from the extreme case, if the Social Intellect of the society is very low, it is possible that one of the thresholds mentioned above is penetrated too much and one of the system breakdown levels is approached. In those cases an over-reactionary jump from the over-dose of one policy directly to the over-dose of the other may occur. Thus the society may oscillate between two extreme policy applications, experiencing very low growth rates one after the other, and consequently ruining its welfare. Such over-reactions are expected to dampen as the society develops some Social Intellect through some heavily damaging experiences.

Next consider a society still with inadequate Social Intellect, but at least got intellectual enough to establish and run a functioning Democracy, such that policy reversals after the over-dose stage of one policy are followed by the initial stage of the alternate policy. Thus, this society can now oscillate on a cycle similar to the one shown in Figure 2.1.B above.

As the Social Intellect of this society increases in time, through accumulating experience while travelling on the cycle, the tolerance of the society to low levels of welfare will decrease, and this will have two consequences. First, by the over-dose stage of the Liberal Policy, the society will not tolerate inequality to rise as much as before, and will react earlier in demanding a policy change. And second, by the over-dose stage of the Social Policy, the society will not tolerate the growth rate to fall as much as before, and again, will react earlier in demanding a policy change[16]. In both cases, therefore, the actual policy change will also come earlier, assuming a well-functioning Democracy.

These changes in timing have significant implications for the average growth rate and the range of inequality during a cycle.

Start with the growth rate. By the over-dose stage of the Social Policy, due to less tolerance for a low growth rate, the minimum growth rate (GR_{MIN} on Figure 2.1.B) at the policy reversal point of Social to Liberal Policy (PC_{LBR}) will increase. Similarly, due to less tolerance for high inequality, the growth rate at the policy reversal point of Liberal to Social Policy (PC_{SCL}) will also increase. As the maximum growth rate (GR_{MAX}) stays the same, the average growth rate during a complete cycle will increase as a consequence of the increase in the Social Intellect of the society.

Next consider the range of inequality. By the over-dose stage of the Liberal Policy, due to less tolerance for high inequality, the maximum inequality (INQ_{MAX} on Figure 2.1.B) at the policy reversal point of Liberal to Social Policy (PC_{SCL}) will decrease towards moderate levels. By the over-dose stage of the Social Policy, due to less tolerance for a low growth rate, the inequality at the policy reversal point of Social to Liberal Policy (PC_{LBR}) will increase towards moderate levels. Therefore, the range of inequality during a complete cycle will narrow down around moderate levels as a consequence of the increase in the Social Intellect of the society.

Considering all together, following the increase in the Social Intellect of the society, the over-dose stages of both polices will be shortened, the average growth rate throughout the cycle will be higher, and the range of inequality throughout the cycle will be narrowed down around moderate levels. Consequently, as has been explained by the end of the previous section, the average welfare throughout the cycle will be higher.

Moreover, as explained above, the lower tolerance for high inequality has decreased the policy reversal threshold level (INQ_{TRH}) at the over-dose stage of Liberal Policy, and the lower tolerance for low growth has increased the policy reversal threshold level (GR_{TRH}) at the over-dose stage of Social Policy. Consequently, the policy reversals at the end of both over-dose policy stages (PC_{SCL} and PC_{LBR}) will occur much earlier than before, thus will stay further away from the dangerous system breakdown levels (INQ_{SYSBRK} and GR_{SYSBRK}), decreasing the danger of a system breakdown. Therefore, the increase in the Social Intellect of the society will also increase the stability of the social order of the society.

As the Social Intellect of the society rises further, the tolerance of the society for high inequality or low growth will decrease further, and the duration of the over-dose stages will also decrease further. Eventually, the society will learn to demand smooth policy changes (reversals) even before the current policies are pushed to their extremes, i.e. just after a decrease in welfare starts from its maximum level in the mature stages. Then, as shown by the dotted lines in Figure 2.1.A, rising Social Intellect will result in changes between moderate policies without going through any over-dose stages. Needles to say, this will further increase the average welfare of the society throughout the cycle.

The next major effect of rising Social Intellect emerges as intellect rises further and actually approaches the adequate levels assumed in principle. Then, the potential establishment of Fair Competition within the economic and political systems of the society will skyrocket the welfare of the society.

Fair Competition

Fair Competition was discussed in detail in Book Two of this series. Again, before discussing the effects of Fair Competition on the welfare of the society, a brief reminder of the relevant basics can be beneficial.

ALLOCATION OF RESOURCES

In both economics and politics, demand and supply meet to form the equilibrium desired by the society. In economics the subject is the availability and pricing of goods and services, in politics it is the rule making (legislation) and the governance (execution). Within this macro picture, each individual plays his micro role. On the demand side, each individual acts as a consumer and a voter. On the supply side, in economics he acts as some sort of supplier of physical or mental labour, and in politics he may act as a Politician.

The macro-equilibrium in both economics and politics forms through a chain of interactions between the individual and the society. *Each individual has personal demand preferences as a consumer and a voter, that are primarily shaped by his Social Intellect.* Individual demands add up to create the society's macro-demand. In turn, the macro-supply of the society forms in reaction to that macro-demand, and each individual adjusts his personal micro-supply to fit into somewhere within that macro-supply. And through this chain reaction the overall equilibrium, and thus the resource allocation within the society, emerges.

To appreciate the scope and the importance of this observation, it will help to clarify what is meant by resources. One easy to guess component of the society's resources is the physical ones. These not only include the natural resources, but also cover labour, thus the physical capacity of a society's human resources. Another easy to guess component is financial resources. But more important are the scientific and technical resources, including the accumulated know-how within the society. And the most important is the mental capacity of the human resources of the society.

As will be discussed soon, the society's welfare will change one way or another depending on where and how these limited resources are allocated. The more intellectual the society gets, the better will be this allocation and consequently the higher will be the society's welfare.

As the allocation of resources is a primary determinant of the welfare of the society, any society will benefit from optimising its resource allocation. And such optimisation requires the demand and supply to meet under conditions of Fair Competition.

FAIR COMPETITION

Fair Competition is a concept beyond free competition, such that it requires the fulfilment of the three conditions below *on both the supply and the demand sides.*

THE FIRST CONDITION

The first condition for Fair Competition is having *a fair opportunity for all competitors in getting prepared for the competition.*

Fair opportunity on the supply side is required to make sure that *all the right candidates should be able to join the competition,* where the term right candidate refers to *those with the highest potential to succeed in competition and thus create the highest value for both the demand side and the society.* Otherwise, a competition among incapables will not result in an optimal distribution of resources.

In particular, *fair opportunity for human resources means that the more capable an individual, the more opportunity he has to be given at both education and employment, solely based on his personal capabilities,* without any practical limitations. In practise, the only way to make sure that more capable individuals reach higher qualified professional positions and optimize the human resource allocation within the society, is to ensure that all markets function under competitive conditions at all times. Under that condition, each corporation has to look for the most capable candidates with the highest professional qualifications, in order to stay competitive and survive in its market.

Regarding the corporate side, fair opportunity primarily means that each corporation can access the necessary financing at rational prices (without paying excessive margins unproportional to their business risks), the necessary know-how (without facing excessively long-lasting and protective intellectual property laws) and the necessary human capital (without facing unfair binding or non-compete clauses that prevent the free movement of human resources).

Fair opportunity on the demand side is required to make sure that all the potential consumers, namely anybody for whom the product has some value, have to be able to reach the market. Otherwise, a limited competition on the demand side will not bring out an optimal price, and thus the mispricing will cause a sub-optimal allocation of resources in the economy.

In practise, for most products, this means that any potential customer should have the purchasing power to join the market, so that the ones who value the product most can demand it. Achieving this, however, necessitates the availability of some basic income for all potential customers, and starts with the prevention of excessive inequality that causes many consumers to lose their purchasing power.

THE SECOND CONDITION

The second condition for Fair Competition is having *free and perfect competition, where all competitors compete under exactly the same rules (and none can effect the making of the rules or can be permitted to violate the rules), there are no barriers to entry or exit, and no single competitor can effect the price formation in the market.*

It is important to emphasize that, on the supply side, for perfect competition, no single producer or group of producers should be able to determine or even effect the price formation in the market, practically meaning that *there must be no concentration of economic power* in the market, let alone the extreme cases of monopolies or oligopolies. For this reason, variations of anti-trust regulations have to be developed and enforced.

Similarly, on the demand side, no single consumer or a group of consumers should be able to determine or even effect the price formation in the market, practically meaning that there must be no monopoly or oligopoly of consumers either. In particular, in the labour market, any monopoly position or concentration of power on the demand side (i.e. the corporate side of the labour market), will mean a loss of value for those individuals who happen to be on the supply side of that labour market, at least in the form of having to accept lower payments and weaker labour rights.

THE THIRD CONDITION

The third condition for Fair Competition is *the existence of proper regulation, to ensure that the rules of competition are set and enforced to protect and promote the long-term interests of the society*[17], *beyond balancing the interests of those who participate in the market as producers on the supply side and as consumers on the demand side.*

Therefore, the society, through its political agents, namely the legislative and executive bodies within the political system, must set the rules and enact regulations such that the society not only wins as a result of the competition defined by those rules and regulations, but also maximises its benefit from that competition by making it a fair one.

SETTING THE RULES OF THE GAME

As all the conditions mentioned above require some degree of regulation to materialize, Fair Competition can only survive in well regulated[18] markets. Regulation, however, is a product of the political system. Therefore, *the optimisation of allocation of resources, which initially seems to depend solely on the well functioning of the economic system, actually requires the well functioning of the political system as well.*

FAIR COMPETITION IN POLITICS

While revisiting the concept of allocation of resources above, it was mentioned that for the optimal allocation of resources within the society, Fair Competition should cover both economics and politics. In the rest of that discussion, however, the explanations were made from the viewpoint of economics. Indeed, from the viewpoint of the economic system, laws and regulations, as products of the political system, are of vital importance. However, that is not the whole story.

It is extremely important to reemphasize that the conditions of Fair Competition should also be valid for the political system. In other words, the competition in politics (covering the political parties, politicians, elections, etc.) should also be based on the conditions of Fair Competition to optimise the allocation of resources within the society. These will be discussed further in Book Four of this series.

FAIR COMPETITION AND SOCIAL INTELLECT

Optimal allocation of resources requires the establishment of Fair Competition, however, the necessary conditions given above are not easy to establish. The adequacy of Social Intellect of the society therefore becomes the primary condition for the proper establishment of these conditions.

In practise, the intellectual level of a society may not be enough to satisfy all these conditions. However, there are always shades of grey between the black and the white, and there are lighter shades versus darker ones, and it is in the best interest of every society to try to get as close as possible to Fair Competition.

Cheating

Cheating was discussed in detail in Book Two of this series, but again, a brief reminder of the relevant basics can be beneficial.

WHAT IS CHEATING

In a Free Market Economy, the primary principle has to be first creating value for the society, and then getting one's fair share of the value created. Although creating value for the society and for oneself simultaneously is the rational and ethical way, it is also the most difficult way. Naturally, some individuals (and corporations) prefer a much easier and faster way, namely cheating.

In simple terms, cheating is to promote one's own interests at the expense of those of the society, by deliberately defying the principles of Fair Competition. Thus, the spread of cheating corresponds to a major decrease in Fair Competition. In a sense, wide spread cheating is the opposite extreme of Fair Competition.

Therefore, within the framework of the ongoing analysis, when Fair Competition is replaced by cheating, the allocation of resources within the society worsens away from the optimal and harms the whole society. The distortion of allocation of resources harms the overall economic growth of the society, while the benefits the Cheaters extract for themselves sharply increases inequality within the society[19].

LACK OF SOCIAL INTELLECT AND WIDESPREAD CHEATING

Widespread cheating is a phenomenon that is seen in societies with low Social Intellect. In such cases, cheating practically violates even the second condition of Fair Competition (namely, free and perfect competition), let alone the first and third conditions.

As cheating spreads in such societies, concentrations of power emerge throughout the economy, and eventually monopolies dominate many markets, eliminating free and perfect competition, and extracting huge benefits for themselves at the expense of the society. At the same time, cheating also spreads in politics, and concentrations of power emerge in the political arena. Soon after, these concentrated powers in the economy and in politics start to cooperate to support and strengthen each other. And all these result in a terrible mis-allocation of resources, decreasing economic growth and increasing inequality.

Effects Of Establishing Fair Competition On The Policy Cycle

Consider the society presented in Section 2.1, whose policy cycle is shown on Figure 2.1.B. As the society passes time on this cycle, it starts to accumulate experience, and eventually starts to increase its Social Intellect.

Initially, the society will realise that it has to minimise cheating as much as possible and thus start to move towards establishing the second condition of Fair Competition (namely, free and perfect competition under the same set of rules). Consequently, it will start to make a better allocation of its resources, and in turn, its growth rate will start to increase and the inequality within the society will start to decrease.

As the society increases its Social Intellect further, it will start to move towards establishing the first and third conditions of Fair Competition as well, and its allocation of resources will improve further.

Before proceeding with the whole journey on rising Social Intellect, it will help to analyse what happens to the policy cycle with the initial increase in the Social Intellect of the society.

A CLOSER LOOK AT THE CHANGES IN INEQUALITY AND GROWTH RATE

First, Fair Competition improves the conditions on both the supply and the demand sides of the economy, and as a consequence, enables a better allocation of resources on both, which in turn increases the economic growth rate. Therefore, *the more a society approaches Fair Competition, the higher will be its economic growth rate.*

Second, through better regulation, including anti-trust laws and treatment of externalities, Fair Competition minimizes cheating and prevents the emergence of concentrations of power within the economy. This will not only result in a better allocation of resources, but also decrease the inequality created by cheating and the concentrations of power.

Third, as fair opportunity in preparation for competition and for employment comes into play, the inequality created by the lack of these will disappear. Needless to say, there will always be winners and losers under Fair Competition as well, as that is what competition is for. However, as nobody is infinitely better than everybody else at all times, as new competitors arrive the winners will change over time. The income of some competitors will still be higher than others, but they will not be extremely higher than everybody else in the long run. Therefore, although Fair Competition still creates inequality, it is not expected to create excessive inequality persistently, but just on the contrary, will annihilate the excessive inequality that emerges at its absence.

Therefore, *the more a society approaches Fair Competition, the more the inequality within the society will approach moderate levels.*

It is important to note that, *decreasing excessive inequality towards moderate levels through the establishment of Fair Competition is a much better way than decreasing excessive inequality through more taxation and redistribution.* This is simply because establishing Fair Competition results in a better allocation of resources (and thus in a higher growth rate), while taxation and redistribution deliberately distort the allocation of resources (and thus decreases the growth rate). Therefore, referring to the discussion at the end of Section 1.3, the society's preference for lower inequality is better realised through establishing Fair Competition. Taxation-and-redistribution should only be kept in mind as the last resort for fine tuning in case Fair Competition is not enough to decrease inequality to the desired levels.

Finally, it goes without saying that, as the Social Intellect of the society improves, it will approach the conditions of Fair Competition not only in the economy, but also in politics. That is to say, fair and free competition in politics will prevent the emergence of concentrations of power in the political arena as well, with all the positive consequences in economics and politics itself. These issues were partially discussed in Books One and Two of this series, and will be discussed in more detail in Book Four.

A CLOSER LOOK AT THE CHANGE IN THE CYCLE

As the discussion above reveals, when the society increases its Social Intellect and improves its economic and political systems towards satisfying the conditions of Fair Competition, the growth rate of the economy increases and the inequality within the society approaches moderate levels. And this will correspond to a shift in the cycle shown in Figure 2.1.B.

From the viewpoint of inequality, as Fair Competition increases, a higher growth rate will be experienced at any given level of inequality, meaning a rightward shift of the cycle.

From the viewpoint of growth rate, as Fair Competition increases, a lower level of inequality will be experienced at any given growth rate, meaning a downward shift of the cycle.

In short, as a combination of these two in practice, when Fair Competition increases, the cycle will shift rightwards (towards higher growth) and downwards (towards lower inequality) on the inequality-growth rate plane.

THE CHANGE IN WELFARE

As discussed in Section 1.3, when the economic growth rate increases while the inequality within the society approaches moderate levels, the welfare of the society increases as a result. Therefore, *the more a society approaches Fair Competition, the higher will be its welfare.*

Overall Effect Of Rising Social Intellect On The Policy Cycle

The analyses presented above in this section revealed that a rise in the Social Intellect of the society has two significant consequences.

First, the society will neither tolerate inequality to rise as much as before by the over-dose stage of the Liberal Policy, nor tolerate the growth rate to fall as much as before by the over-dose stage of the Social Policy. Consequently, it will react earlier in both cases in demanding a policy change, and assuming a well functioning Democracy, the actual policy changes will come earlier than before.

Second, through minimising cheating and establishing Fair Competition, it makes a better allocation of resources, and consequently gets an improved inequality versus economic growth dynamic.

And regarding the policy cycle, the first curbs the extremes of the cycle, and the second shifts the cycle rightwards and downwards.

To visualise the overall effect of rising Social Intellect, consider two different societies. The first society has low Social Intellect and thus oscillates on the cycle presented on Figure 2.1.B. The second society has a higher Social Intellect and therefore has a different cycle, curbed at the extremes and shifted rightwards and downwards. The cycles of these two societies are presented together on Figure 2.2.A.

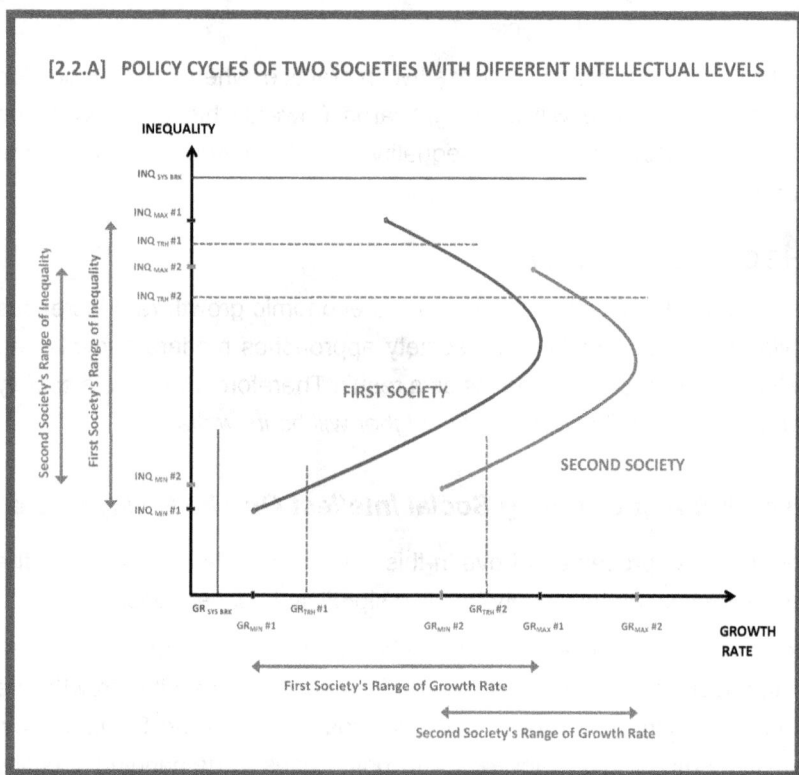

[2.2.A]   POLICY CYCLES OF TWO SOCIETIES WITH DIFFERENT INTELLECTUAL LEVELS

The figure reveals the significant consequences of rising Social Intellect:

From the viewpoint of economic growth, the second society has a higher average growth rate throughout its cycle, thus resulting in a higher economic growth in the long run. This is a combined result of the facts that, both the maximum growth rate attained by the second society is higher due to a better allocation of resources, and the minimum growth rates attained by the society are also higher due to curbing the extremes. Therefore, one significant conclusion is that, *the higher the Social Intellect of the society, the higher will be its economic growth in the long run*.

As the maximum growth rate attained by the society is higher, it directly follows that the maximum welfare level attained around the moderate inequality level is also higher. Moreover, the second society has a narrower range of inequality around the moderate levels as a result of curbing the extremes during the over-dose stages. Remembering that the welfare of the society falls to its minimum levels at the extremes, when the extremes are curbed the range of change in welfare around its maximum level within the cycle is narrower as well. Again, as both the maximum and minimum welfare levels have risen, the average welfare for the society during the cycle has also risen. Therefore, another significant conclusion is that, *the higher the Social Intellect of the society, the higher will be its welfare.*

Finally, as the extremes at the over-dose stages are curbed, and the cycle has shifted rightwards and downwards, the policy changes in the second society occur much earlier (than the policy changes in the first society), thus staying further away from the system breakdown levels at both extremes. In other words, the second society will react to a rise in inequality way before the inequality system breakdown level (INQ_{SYSBRK}) is approached during the over-dose stage of the Liberal Policy, and to a fall in growth rate way before the growth rate system breakdown level (GR_{SYSBRK}) is approached during the over-dose stage of the Social Policy. Therefore, the final significant conclusion is that, *the higher the Social Intellect of the society, the higher will be the stability of its economic and political systems.*

Travelling Towards Optimal Policy And Optimum Welfare

In the sub-section above, the cycles of two separate societies with different intellectual levels are compared. In practise, a society does not jump from one Social Intellect level to another higher one instantaneously, but rather develops its Social Intellect gradually as it gains experience with every policy cycle it goes through. Therefore, the development of the cycles of a society with rising Social Intellect have a continuous pattern in practice, as shown on Figure 2.2.B.

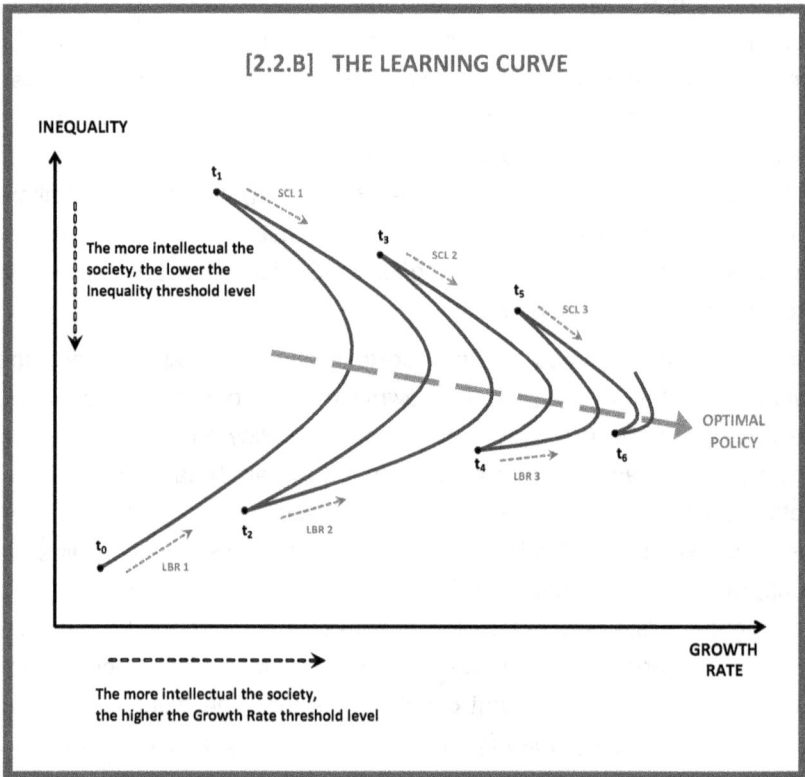

INTELLECT AND EXPERIENCE

As a society develops its Social Intellect, policy reversals are demanded earlier and Fair Competition is better established, increasing both its economic growth and welfare, as discussed above.

Increasing Social Intellect, however, is not a trivial matter. As discussed in Book One of this series, a fast rise in Social Intellect requires a heavy investment in a well designed social education program for all the members of the society, but this is naturally not demanded by a society when its Social Intellect is low to begin with. Fortunately, although slower and less efficient than education, accumulating experience also rises the Social Intellect of a society in time, as the society oscillates between one economic policy and the other. Considering that each policy cycle takes many years to complete, this learning through trial and error process takes much longer compared to increasing the intellectual level of the society through some social education, but at least it works without a need for any deliberate action. Even better, it works in spite of any potential deliberate attempts of some Cheaters to prevent such an improvement in the Social Intellect of the society, as discussed in Book Two.

As the society gathers experience through each cycle, it will learn to demand policy reversals earlier at the over-dose phases of each policy. More importantly, it will learn to demand the establishment of not only the second but also the third and first conditions of Fair Competition in the markets - usually in that order. This gradual improvement from one policy cycle to the next can be defined as *travelling on the learning curve*.

Thanks to its accumulation of experience, the society will learn to modify both policies for the better after each cycle. Each policy will integrate the preceding one's best attributes[20], curb its own extremes and thus will continuously transform itself for the better, increasing the society's welfare throughout the journey.

TRAVELLING ON THE LEARNING CURVE

As shown on Figure 2.2.B, at the very beginning of the cycles, both the Liberal and Social Policies are at their most extreme versions, as both policies initially materialize as reactions to each others' exaggerations and weaknesses, rather than being based on rational thinking. The society is at the beginning of its learning curve by definition, thus society's intellectual level is at its lowest compared to its future potential development. As the society experiences both policies alternatively

(LBR-1 and SCL-1) and thus travels on its learning curve, it becomes more intellectual, and both curbs the extremes and starts to apply conditions of Fair Competition during the next cycle (LBR-2 and SCL-2). As its intellect improves further, the process gets even better in the following cycle (LBR-3 and SCL-3). Eventually, as both policies get milder and share more common approaches with each other, the variation between Social and Liberal Policies is minimized and the society approaches to its own *Optimal Policy*, under the prevailing conditions.

At each cycle of this journey towards the Optimal Policy, the average growth rate increases, the range of inequality narrows around moderate levels, and consequently the welfare of the society increases, as shown in Figure 2.2.C. Eventually, as the Optimal Policy is approached, the welfare of the society is also optimised, reaching its *long-term maximum level*.

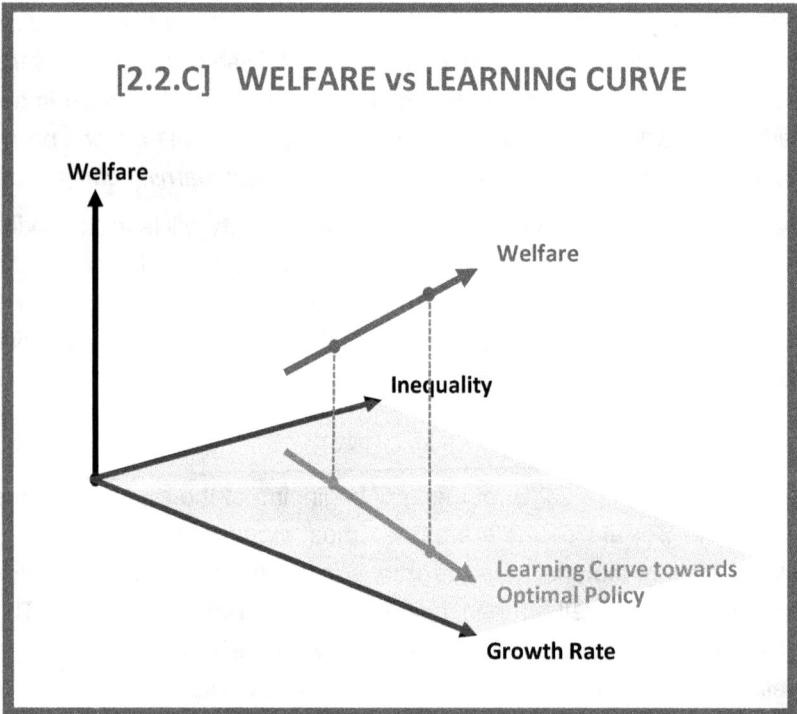

[2.2.C] WELFARE vs LEARNING CURVE

It is important to reemphasize that, each society has a different and unique set of cultural characteristics, and therefore a different Optimal Policy that will optimise their welfare. Therefore, the Optimal Policy solution for one society will not fit to another. In other words, each society has to travel on its own learning curve to search for its own Optimal Policy, rather than trying to copy others' solutions blindly. For instance, continental Europe prefers policies with more of a social emphasis, while the United States prefer policies with more of a liberal emphasis, both based on their cultures and historical experiences. However, the dynamics of the travel on the learning curve is still similar for all.

THE SPEED OF TRAVEL THROUGH POLICY CYCLES

Different societies not only have different Optimal Policies, but have different speeds of developing Social Intellect and travelling through the cycles on their own learning curve. In other words, the speed of progress at each stage of each policy, and therefore the time spent in that stage, varies from policy to policy, cycle to cycle, and society to society. The period for each complete cycle is thus different for each society at different times.

In general, the lower the Social Intellect of a society, the more time it spends for a complete cycle, simply because its demands for policy changes arise too late during the over-dose stages of each policy. In other words, its over-dose stages may last too long. As its intellectual level rises, the over-dose stages will shorten, and even totally disappear in the late cycles, speeding up the travel on the learning curve.

For an illustrative example, refer to the graphic next, depicting the policy shifts and changes in two different societies, say A and B.

[2.2.D]   POLICY CYCLES : Stages, Shifts, Changes - an illustration

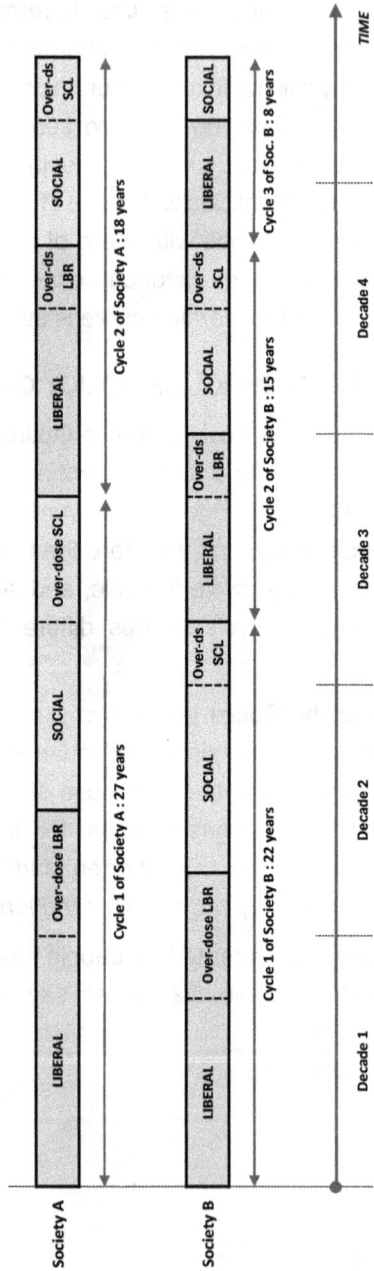

- And there are very many further technological advances unimaginable now, like those in artificial intelligence and quantum computing, that can be considered as major game changers by themselves, coming soon.

GLOBALISATION

The second major game changer is globalisation. Again, to illustrate some effects:

- Free flow of goods and services resulted in trade imbalances between societies, transferring wealth from one to the other, while within many societies the fruits of the resulting economic growth was not shared fairly, increasing inequality,
- Free flow of labour resulted in both immigration and the moving of production facilities to other societies, and the resulting increase in profitability of global corporations due to utilizing cheap labour was not shared by the domestic labour through any new social policies, increasing inequality at economically developed societies,
- Free flow of capital, through the global banking and credit systems, enabled a flow from societies with trade surpluses to those with deficits, hiding the rising income inequality behind debt-financed consumption in the receiving end, delaying any potential demand for a policy change,
- Corporate activities with a global span, merged many markets into one single global market and created global monopolies with excessive profits, while decreasing competition at the expense of both the consumers and the labour.

Global integration, if structured properly (as will be discussed in another book of this series), can be beneficial in both decreasing inequality globally and increasing growth rate of all societies, increasing global welfare. However, when handled improperly, as done in the recent decades, it may rise inequality in almost every society, while decreasing competition as a result of creating global monopolies, consequently decreasing welfare everywhere. The right solution, is not giving up on global integration, but to travel on a new learning curve, improve the lost (or never before developed) Social Intellect first, and then implement global integration properly, such that welfare will rise everywhere.

THE POTENTIAL SHOWER OF GAME CHANGERS ON HORIZON

The two game changers mentioned above are just the beginning of a potential shower of others in the coming decades. There are many more on the horizon, some partially recognized, some totally unimagined by now. For instance, global warming and depleting natural resources can be one. A global political crisis resulting in a bi-polar or tri-polar global order can be another, as the United States gives up, or -for primarily economic reasons- has to retreat from, its big-brother role in the almost unipolar world of the past decades. The unfortunate fact is that, the more the societies lose relative Social Intellect on the already arrived game changers, the worse they will be caught with inadequate Social Intellect to the potential game changers. The clear trouble, therefore, is the danger of a system breakdown that may consequently result in a highly damaging chaos.

Stability And A Closer Look

The re-starting of a new learning curve following the arrival of a major game changer, and finding the New Optimal Policy for the society is a natural dynamic of the system. However, following this dynamic does not ensure that either the end-result will be better or the journey on the learning curve will be safe.

First, the new optimal welfare at the New Optimal Policy may or may not be better than the previous optimal welfare. If it comes out to be better, all will be fine. But if it is worse, by the time the society re-develops its Social Intellect and realizes that the game changer was not supposed to happen in the first place -as it caused a decrease in its welfare-, it is usually too late to reverse the game changer. Furthermore, the real danger here is that, if the eventual new inequality level or the new growth rate resulting from the New Optimal Policy happens to violate either of the system breakdown levels (too high inequality or too low growth), the society may experience a social upheaval, lose its social order and end up in chaos, as mentioned above. And then what comes next is unforecastable.

For instance, if the society jumps on artificial intelligence without analysing the potential consequences, where it ends up after the implementation of such technologies will be a matter of luck at best. And if the end result is not loved afterwards, it will be too late to reverse the process. A similar argument can be made regarding the emergence of global warming and the global society's ignoring it – when the eventual outcome of neglecting adverse developments today clarifies in the future, it may be too late to reverse the process. Many other cases can be found with the common denominator that the Social Intellect of the society becomes or remains inadequate to handle the game changer properly in time.

Second, even if the eventual new optimal welfare at the New Optimal Policy will be above the previous optimal welfare, and that the game changer will come out to be beneficial for the society, still, as the journey on the new learning curve starts way behind the optimal and initially has huge swings between policies, one of the system breakdown levels can be violated during the travel on the new learning curve, again resulting in chaos on the way, before being able to complete the new learning curve.

In other words, even the game changers that will increase the welfare of the society in the long run when the Optimal Policy is discovered, may initially decrease welfare when the society falls back on the learning curve at the very beginning of its journey. Thus, on the welfare front, things may get worse in the short run even if they may get better in the long run. The danger here is that, if the welfare level falls too much during the journey, due to either a too high inequality level or a too low economic growth, then a system breakdown can occur on the way, before the Optimal Policy can be discovered.

A good illustration of this case is the globalisation experienced during the recent decades. As explained above, even though global integration will benefit all societies when handled in the right way (i.e. when the New Optimal Policy is discovered by most societies), it may have too adverse effects during the travel on the learning curve (due to the extreme weakening of Social Intellect) that may cause significant instability within or between societies. Indeed, there is a drawback from globalisation following its fast spread for a couple of decades, which will hopefully enable the societies to recover some Social Intellect first and then restructure global integration in a much beneficial way for all societies.

In short, it is existentially important for a society to take all the precautions to prevent a too heavy fall in its Social Intellect when a major game changer eventually arrives, such that any inevitable fall back on the new learning curve can be contained within boundaries that do not result in any violation of the system breakdown levels and cause any sort of social upheaval that may ruin the social order.

What Should The Society Do

In principle, the best way to prevent a system breakdown is improving the Social Intellect of the society such that it leads the potential game changers rather than lagging behind them. Or, in cases where a lag is inevitable, at least prevent its Social Intellect from falling too far behind. This way, the society can prevent both the emergence of a potentially harmful game changer, and the extremely wide swings in policies at the beginning of the new learning curve in cases where the game changer will eventually benefit the society.

In practise, however, when the process of developing Social intellect is primarily based on trial-and-error (i.e. experiencing the changes *after* the game changer arrives) as is the case today, then, let alone leading the game changer, even preventing a too heavy fall back is difficult by definition.

Leading the game changer, or at least preventing a heavy fall back of Social Intellect, can only happen if a wide spread social education system is established, and supported with accurate and timely information flow for sustaining the society's social awareness – as explained in detail in Book One of this series.

This way the society can keep its capacity to re-travel on the new learning curve faster and without falling too many cycles behind its New Optimal

Policy, consequently keeping its welfare at higher levels throughout the journey and not facing the risk of a system breakdown.

In short, it is vital to keep the Social Intellect and awareness of the society as high as possible to survive through the continuous arrival of major game changers. However, rather than deliberately trying hard to do so, the society unknowingly loses, or worse, is deliberately made to lose, its Social Intellect and social awareness in practise, as will be discussed in the next chapter.

CHAPTER 3

WHEN DOES DEMOCRACY FAIL TO REBALANCE THE SYSTEM ?

3.1   From Theory To Practise

In Chapter 2, a theoretical simple model based on the concepts analysed in Books One and Two of this series was introduced. It has explained how societies travel on a learning curve towards their Optimal Policy and optimal welfare, as they develop their Social Intellect.

APPLICATION OF THE THEORY TO PRACTICE

By the middle of the 20th century, the societies on the two coasts of the Atlantic Ocean resembled Society Two within the framework of Section 2.2, specifically referring to Figure 2.2.A. They have already developed some Social Intellect, thus had lower thresholds for inequality and economic growth relative to the previous decades, however, they were still swinging between liberal and social policies that are significantly different from each other. Thus, they were still away from their optimal policies.

When the major game changers discussed in Section 2.3 (namely, technological advancements and globalisation) have arrived by the second half of the 20th century, they have created a more complex environment, and caused the already inadequate Social Intellect of these societies to weaken further, and placed these societies far away from their new optimal policies (to the initial cycles of a new learning curve), within the framework of Section 2.2, referring to Figure 2.2.B.

Consequently, by the beginning of the 21st century, the critical question was whether these societies could resume travelling on their new learning curves towards their new optimal policies at an adequate speed or not. Unfortunately, the answer seems to be negative for the time being.

In this chapter, more of the issues presented in Books One and Two of this series will be combined to analyse why these societies are experiencing a delay in starting their journey on their new learning curves, let alone attaining a satisfactory speed of progress. In other words, Chapter 3 will examine why, in practise, these societies are not behaving in the way the theory assumes.

3.2   The Check-And-Balance Relation Between Economics And Politics - Revisited

As discussed in the previous chapters, the western social order based on Free Market Economy and Democracy assumes that there is a *check-and-balance relation between economics and politics*, such that, when some trouble emerges in the economy, a political reaction arises and results in a policy change that cures the trouble. In other words, *there is an implicit assumption that economic developments will have political consequences*.

More precisely, *if inequality rises or growth rate falls too much beyond the respective tolerance levels of the society* (called *thresholds* in the jargon of the previous chapter), and consequently the welfare of the society decreases towards minimum levels, *a political reaction should arise*.

The tolerance levels of the society, in turn, are *inversely related* to the Social Intellect of the society: *the higher the Social Intellect, the lower the tolerance for a rise in inequality or a fall in growth rate – and vice versa*.

From time to time, significant *game changers* emerge, such that inequality rises or growth rate falls too much as their consequence, and then the society starts to travel on *a new learning curve* to find out *a new Optimal Policy* to tackle these changes and cure the troubles in the economy.

In short, in any case and at any time, there has to be some tolerance levels regarding the economic troubles, beyond which the society should give a political reaction and demand a change in policies to cure such troubles within a rational time frame.

How come, then, through the recent decades, even in the western societies, when inequality rises and/or growth rate falls too much, the check-and-balance relation between economics and politics fails to function to cure the troubles?

THE STRANGE CASE OF PERSISTENT HIGH INEQUALITY

High inequality, in essence, means that those on the winning side of the inequality experience an economic growth much higher than the average of the society, while those on the losing side experience an economic growth much lower than the average of the society.

Therefore, those on the losing side experience not only inequality rising against themselves, but also too low (or even negative) economic growth. In other words, they simultaneously experience two troubles either of which is expected to create some political reaction. Consequently, under these conditions, even if their intellectual level is inadequate (or has fallen below the adequate level), they should still show some political reaction without too much of a delay.

And when the political system is a Democracy, which is based on *absolute political equality* (through the one-man-one-vote principle), this reaction should immediately turn into a widespread and strong political demand, consequently resulting in a policy change within a short period of time – say a few years[21].

Therefore, too high inequality should not last too long within the check-and-balance dynamic of the western social order. How come, then, many western societies are witnessing the strange co-existence of too high inequality and Democracy in practise, although they are mutually exclusive in theory?

FUNDAMENTAL REASONS OF FAILURE

The persistence of high economic inequality within a political system built on absolute equality is an anomaly. Similarly, the persistence of low economic growth within a political system that enables the transformation of political demand to a policy change within a rational time frame is another anomaly. These strange cases where the theory fails in practise, are consequences of two fundamental reasons: *the shift of attention to non-economic issues within politics* and *the shift of attention away from politics*.

3.3   Shift Of Attention To Non-Economic Issues Within Politics

The cases where the attention of the society shifts from economic issues to non-economic ones within politics constitute the first set of fundamental reasons where practice diverges from theory. In all the cases analysed below, the check-and-balance relation between economics and politics fails to function in the way assumed in theory.

Any one of the cases below has the potential to break or weaken the check-and-balance relation by itself, but to make matters worse, they are not mutually exclusive, and consequently many of them may simultaneously emerge and exist in practise.

Approaching Optimal Policy

If the society can develop its Social Intellect and travel on its learning curve for long enough without interruption, the liberal and social economic policies will converge to reveal the Optimal Policy under the prevailing conditions of the day, and will stabilise there, as explained in Section 2.2. If the society approaches this Optimal Policy, inequality will be at moderate levels, growth rate will be high, economic troubles will be minimised, and consequently the welfare of the society will be at its highest level within the last couple of decades. It will feel like finding heaven on earth.

Unfortunately, *as a result of this stability at this very high welfare level, the attention of the society will naturally and easily shift away from the economy, and political considerations will start to focus on other non-economic issues.*

In time, even at the absence of any major game changers, effects of several medium sized changes will accumulate in the background without being noticed, and slowly increase the complexity of the environment. Consequently, the Social Intellect of the society will fall slowly against this gradually rising complexity, while the society will stay unaware of this negative progress for a long time. In the meantime, there will be a slow but persistent trend of either an increase in inequality or a decrease in growth rate, and the welfare of the society will slowly deteriorate.

Finally, someday either the high inequality or the low growth rate threshold will be so much violated that the situation will re-attract the society's attention. But unfortunately, by then the society will lack the necessary Social Intellect to analyse the situation correctly and find the cure shortly.

In the best case, the society escapes a system breakdown and eventually starts to re-travel on a new learning curve, albeit at some point so far away from the new Optimal Policy that it will need a long time on the way before it can restore its lost welfare level.

And in the worst case, it may be too late to prevent a system breakdown when the society eventually wakes up, and a long period of chaos may follow. This usually happens when a major game changer arrives when the Social Intellect of the society has already weakened significantly, and thus the major game changer becomes the final nail on the coffin.

Mis-Analysing The Causes, Consequences And Cures Of A Major Game Changer

When a major game changer emerges, even just after an Optimal Policy is approached and thus the Social Intellect of the society has not weakened much, the society experiences a sudden major fall in its Social Intellect relative to this new high-complexity of the environment, as discussed in Section 2.3. The economic troubles that arise as a result of the arrival of this major game changer will then start to decrease the welfare of the society in a short time - relative to the time the society needs to regain its lost intellect.

In many such cases, *the abrupt weakening of its Social Intellect will cause the society to fail to see the real causation relations[22] behind the newly emerged economic troubles and mis-diagnose the sources and thus the cure of these troubles.* And on several occasions of this sort, instead of focusing on economic issues, the society's attention shifts to non-economic issues which may seem to be relevant on the surface, but actually not among the main causes at all. This way, the society concentrates its attention on marginally related non-economic issues in search for a cure, consequently delaying the diagnosis of the real economic cause and the implementation of the appropriate cure, and letting the uncured trouble get even worse in the meantime.

For instance, as it has happened during the recent decades, the inequality in an economically-developed western society may be rising against some segments of labour due to rising automation (as a result of technological advancements) and shifting of production to other societies where labour is much cheaper (as a result of globalisation). But if the society happens to think that the primary cause of the trouble is immigration (and the arrival of cheap labour as a result of it) and develops a primarily nationalistic response against foreigners, and spends valuable time on focusing on limiting immigration -which only has a marginal effect on the economic trouble-, the trouble naturally continues to worsen in the background without being cured.

In this case, the non-economic issue, namely the trouble with immigration, is supported and strengthened by other side issues, like the dilution of the local culture as a result of heavy immigration. Although there definitely is some truth in this argument, it is not relevant to the main economic trouble, which is the rise in inequality in the society. However, this side issue further distracts attention away from the primary trouble which is economic, towards a secondary issue that is non-economic.

To get a feel of the real priority ranking of the society regarding these issues, consider the case where the immigration of foreigners, say the well educated professionals or wealthy ones, actually fuels the economic growth of the society and benefits everyone. Clearly, there is no nationalistic reaction towards immigration of that sort – even though the dilution of the local culture is still a valid fact. Indeed, even the nationalistic politicians conveniently distinguish between the immigration of the poor unqualified labour (which economically hurts the locals) versus the immigration of the well-educated or the wealthy (which benefits everyone). Therefore, the dilution of culture is of secondary priority and is clearly dominated by the economic effect of immigration.

Going back to the main economic trouble, namely the rise in inequality, a better diagnosis would bring forward the issues regarding technological advancements and globalisation, both of which are of economic nature in essence, and neither of which is treated properly. Therefore, attention has to focus on these economic issues, and until a cure is found and new policies are set, some temporary additional taxation-and-distribution system can be established, such that the extreme winners of high-tech and globalisation are further taxed to aid the losers. But focusing on immigration alone is just a distraction of attention and does not cure the main trouble.

To repeat, when major game changers emerge and the society experiences a major fall in its Social Intellect, it may fail to see the real reasons behind its new economic troubles, and may try to find a solution by focusing on barely relevant non-economic issues, letting the uncured trouble get even worse.

Again, if the society is lucky, it will shift its attention to economic issues before it faces a system breakdown.

The Artificial Promotion Of Non-Economic Issues

CASES OF LACK OF GOODWILL

At times when the Social Intellect of the society is weakened within an environment of rising complexity, some politicians and/or some concentrated economic powers (as discussed in Book Two) may try to utilise this opportunity to their own benefit at the expense of the society, through distracting the attention of the society away from the real economic troubles to artificial non-economic issues that are barely relevant (if at all) to the real economic issue.

As the effects of many individually minor changes accumulate to rise the complexity of the environment gradually, and then major game changers emerge to further complicate the situation, the society experiences a significant weakening of its Social Intellect. This creates the perfect environment for the emergence of the populist politicians and policies.

One common approach is transforming the economic issue to a marginally relevant non-economic one that is easier to communicate and faster to solve. As discussed in detail in Book One of this series, *any major economic issue that requires deep analysis and demanding long-term solutions, which makes it difficult to understand and painful to accept, is an opportunity for the populist politician to create misconceptions utilising non-economic issues, and present some shallow (and naturally wrong) analysis with simple (but useless) short-term solutions.*

Another common approach is *promoting some non-economic issue, or artificially creating one, where the populist politician considers himself politically stronger and his policies more attractive than those of his rivals', to the level of an existential significance for the society.* He distracts attention away from all the other major issues (including the economic ones) that are actually much more significant, and tries to focus the attention of the society on the issue he is promoting. The society is made to believe that solving that non-economic issue has to be prioritised, as it is much more important and urgent than any other economic trouble, and thus the society has to make its political decisions accordingly, practically meaning that it has to vote for the populist politician.

Deliberate distraction of attention away from the economic issues to non-economic ones to serve private interests is not a phenomenon limited to the political arena. Actually, an even stronger effort comes from the economic side. As discussed in Book Two of this series, many concentrated interest groups in the economy deliberately push forward non-economic issues above the attention level they would naturally attract, at all times, so that they can run their own economic agendas, to their own interest at the expense of the rest of the society, without being noticed by the society. This way, they can either prevent the implementation of the cure for the economic trouble that benefits them, or at least delay the cure as long as possible. And to achieve that, these concentrated interest groups may cooperate with the politicians who will support the policies that will be beneficial for the interest group.

All these approaches to distract attention away from economic issues by the politicians (and the concentrated interest groups cooperating with them at times) for their own benefit at the expense of the society, should be considered as cheating against the society and thus as signs of lack of goodwill[23].

However, strangely enough, not all the politicians who revert to populist rhetoric necessarily lack goodwill.

GOODWILLED POLITICIANS DESPERATELY REVERTING TO POPULISM

If the Social Intellect of the society has weakened so much that, a major economic trouble, and its causes and cures, can not be easily and clearly communicated with the society, then the Politicians may have to revert to simple non-economic messages and deliberately distract the attention of the society, not because of their lack of goodwill, but because they have no other choice left to win the political support of the society.

As discussed in Book Two of this series, by applying the basic concepts of economics to politics, it can be said that economic and social policies are the products of a Politician that he aims to sell to the society and get paid in return by receiving their political support (namely, votes). In this regard, *any political opinion has to be marketable to the society in order to attract political support*.

A marketable opinion, in turn, has to have two attributes. First, it should be *understandable* with respect to the adequacy of the Social Intellect of the society. And second, it should be *likeable* if and when understood.

Unfortunately but naturally, in the complex environment of our day, many major economic troubles, and their causes and remedies, happen to be complex. Moreover, they mostly require short-term sacrifices for long-term benefits. Therefore, they are neither easily understandable nor much likeable, and fail to satisfy both of the above conditions for marketability.

In light of this unfortunate fact, *if a Politician insists on giving the right messages and making the right promises, which means presenting the complex, painful but correct long-term solutions, he simply can not get sufficient political support to win an election and apply his policies – in spite of his ability to properly analyse the trouble and the cure, and his goodwill.*

Consequently, in cases where the society has lost too much Social Intellect, Politicians have no choice but to change and simplify their opinions and promises on policies such that they become understandable and likeable, at times including a deliberate diversion of attention to barely relevant non-economic issues that can be more easily communicated. However, such simplifications and diversions may make their policies and their practical implementations inadequate, and unfortunately, that is a price the society will have to pay for losing its Social intellect.

In short, *the primary flaw within the western social order is that, many Politicians who are actually capable, sincere and ethical, are forced by the inadequacy of the Social Intellect of the society to revert to marketable populist approaches – that will at best be a partial solution for the main economic trouble.*

Therefore, as was discussed in the previous books and will be discussed again in Book Four of this series, *in a Democracy no one can save the society unless the society develops and sustains adequate Social Intellect to demand to be saved by rational policies instead of following populist promises.*

A SIMPLE ILLUSTRATIVE CASE : GLOBALISATION AND THE USA

By the last decades of the 20th century, enjoying its unipolar power status, the United States itself has created and structured the global order that introduced free trade and free flow of capital. However, ever since, it has been suffering huge trade deficits that benefitted the far eastern societies and practically caused a transfer of wealth from the US to those societies. More specifically, that global order has caused a transfer of wealth from the US labour to the cheap labour in those societies. To make matters worse, those far eastern societies has saved their trade surpluses, and through buying US debt, financed the consumption of the US consumers, which increased the trade deficit further and started a vicious cycle. As both the trade deficit and the foreign borrowing of the US is continuously rising, the sustainability of this cycle is becoming more and more difficult, and consequently the necessity for a significant structural change is clear.

One interesting question here is that, if this global order is hurting the US, why had it established that order in the first place? The answer is in the details of a complex structure: the concentrated economic powers in the US had originally guided the politicians to establish such a flawed global order, as their costs of production utilising the cheap labour in the far eastern societies is significantly lower, and thus their corporate profits are significantly higher under that scheme. However, as these corporations build their fortunes within this global order, the US society has paid the price through a transfer of wealth in the form of trade deficits. And within the society, the labour working in the production of tradeable goods have been hurt most. Moreover, the benefits of the globalisation of this sort that have primarily been taken by the major corporations were mostly kept out overseas to escape taxation, and thus, not shared much with the rest of the US society in any way – as, by avoiding taxation these have not helped to finance any potential government spending or further social security measures at home. To make matters worse, as the financing from the far eastern societies that enjoy the trade surpluses has enabled further consumption of the US society, the rising income inequality against most of the society in the US is hidden behind the sustained -or even amplified (based on lower prices)- consumption. Consequently, the US society has failed to notice the trouble with this flawed global order and its harm to itself until the 2008 crisis hit[24].

Up to this point, this flawed global structure is a case of a major game changer with negative consequences. Unfortunately, what happened, or better to say, what has not happened afterwards, is worse – but still within the framework introduced in the previous chapters and sections.

The right response for the 2008 crisis should have been starting the re-structuring of the flawed global free trade order in the right way for the long run (such that both the US trade deficit and the financing of it by the trade surpluses of the far eastern societies should be curbed), while simultaneously, some temporary taxation-and-distribution has to be done in the short run to rapidly decrease the inequality that arose due to the unfair sharing of the benefits of globalisation within the US society.

The critical observation in this illustrative case is that, even in this over-simplified form, the trouble in the economy, the causation relations behind it, and thus the cure for it are too complicated to be communicated effectively with the masses who have already lost some Social Intellect as a result of the game changer (flawed globalisation) itself.

Therefore, there is an unfortunate need to express the trouble and the cure in much simpler and preferably easily understandable non-economic terms. One practical way of doing that is naturally reverting to simple nationalistic arguments that are both easy to communicate with the society and effective in receiving its political support.

TWO CRITICAL QUESTIONS

This case, or any case like this, brings two significant questions.

The first question is, whether such a nationalistic approach, or any other similar distractions of attention to other non-economic issues, is utilised as a convenient tool by some populist politician trying to serve his own political interests, or is it a goodwilled approach needed to create a much-simplified message to guide the society in the right direction towards the real cure without waiting for (and risking) a long and dangerous walk on a new learning curve.

And the second question is, even if the answer to the first question is the arrival of the goodwilled politician, whether the ability of the politician is adequate, and thus the hidden cure in his mind is correct in principle and can be implemented properly in practise.

If the answers to both of the questions above are positive, then all will be fine for this lucky society both in the short and in the long run: on the one hand, it will be implementing the necessary remedies to solve its economic troubles, on the other hand, it will re-develop its Social Intellect on the way without facing any risks of a system breakdown.

However, if one of the answers to the questions above is negative, then the implementation of a deliberate or goodwilled wrong cure, will not only fail to cure the existing economic troubles, but will also introduce further new economic or social troubles, increasing the risk of a system breakdown on the way. In other words, instead of guiding the society towards the new Optimal Policy, the wrong cure will push the society further away towards amplified oscillations between potentially extreme applications of liberal and social policies.

Therefore, the more rational and less dangerous solution is always rising and sustaining the Social Intellect of the society as much as possible at all times, so that even in cases of arrivals of major game changers, the weakening of its intellect will be limited, and consequently, the real troubles, their real causes and cures can be communicated without any need for unnecessary simplifications or diversions to marginally relevant non-economic issues. This way, neither any goodwilled politicians will need to deliberately over-simplify the troubles and the cures or distract the attention to marginally relevant non-economic issues to gain political support, nor any cheating politician will have the opportunity to benefit himself through populist approaches.

Existence Of A Too Strong Social Security System

The social security system of a society has a more significant effect on the inequality and economic growth -and thus on the welfare- of the society than commonly recognized. When applied at an optimal dose, social security can help to maximise the welfare of the society, while both its under-dose and over-dose have negative consequences. For that reason, the next chapter in this book is completely allocated to the discussion of social security. However, for the sake of the completeness of the discussion in this section, some relevant issues will be briefly presented next.

Contrary to the common belief, when there is a too strong and widespread social security for those individuals at the working age (in the form of unemployment insurance or aid or else) and the elderly (in the form of retirement pensions or benefits or else), the social order of the society can be negatively effected in the long run in many ways - two of which are related to the discussion in this section.

First, a too strong social security will practically isolate the financial wellbeing of the benefiters from the economic developments. A too strong unemployment insurance will significantly decrease the risk that anyone at the working ages may face on a personal basis at times of low economic growth. A too strong pension plan similarly isolates the elderly from the performance of the economy. Consequently, it will be easier for both groups, who happen to be the dominant part of the voting base in any Democracy, to have less interest in economic developments and let their attention be distracted to non-economic or even non-political issues.

Second, as long as an over-dosed social security system is in place, both these groups will naively believe that the system will last forever without interruption, independent of whatever happens in the economy, and thus they don't need to care too much about the economic issues. Unfortunately, as the societies age and birthrates fall simultaneously as a result of the ongoing trend in the latest decades, the number of those at working ages (who are supposed to finance the pensions of the elderly by the taxes they pay) decrease, while the number of the elderly increase. Consequently, the burden on the social security system rises while the source of financing falls, further endangering the delicate balances in the social security system every passing day. Within this environment, if the income inequality rises for any reason, more people at working ages will sooner or later need social aid, increasing the burden on the system further and faster. Alternatively, if the growth rate falls for some reason, the taxes collected will fall and the financing of the social security system will be hurt, again endangering the system further and faster. In any case, the social security system may collapse (or at least has to be weakened) at the expense of the benefiters someday. Therefore, the benefiters of a strong social security system should better not lose interest in the economic developments as they make their political choices. Unfortunately, the mis-belief for the eternal sustainability of the strong social security system results in just the opposite.

In short, *a too strong and widespread social security system, together with the mis-belief on its sustainability, makes many individuals in the society feel that their financial wellbeing will not be effected much by the developments in the economy, and thus they may enjoy the luxury to distract their attention to non-economic issues.* Unfortunately, such a mistake resulting from the weakening of the Social Intellect of the society may hurt its welfare significantly – even in the medium run.

The Rise Of The Cultural And Social Dimension In Politics

The analysis of the dynamics of Free Market Economy and Democracy presented in Chapter 2 assumes that politics is shaped primarily by economics, such that the political parties defending liberal policies are on one side and the political parties defending social policies are on the other, and that the society shifts its economic preferences between these two economic policies. This explicit assumption actually includes the hidden implicit assumption that, the society is somewhat homogeneous in its cultural and social dimension, so that politics is primarily shaped by economics rather than other non-economic issues.

And that used to be the case in practise in the western societies, until the two major game changers mentioned in Section 2.3 arrived.

One of these major game changers is the rise of globalisation, including the free flow of labour which helped to fuel immigration and a flow of foreign culture and social norms with it.

The other major game changer is the developments in communication technologies that enabled the sharing of diverse opinions, thoughts and cultural values globally, exposing the young generations (and some older ones) to many different social and political views, preferences and expectations.

These two major changes together have converted the once culturally and socially homogenous western societies to heterogenous ones.

Finally, to pour fuel to the fire, the rise of intellectual inequality within the societies (as will be defined and discussed in Section 3.5), arising from the significant differences in levels of education and Social Intellect among the members of the societies, has further increased cultural and social heterogeneity.

Consequently, on the political front, in the heterogeneous societies of our day, on the one hand, people with the same nationality, race, religious beliefs etc may have very diverse opinions on social issues and may not feel close to each other at all, while, on the other hand, people with different nationalities, races, religious beliefs etc may have similar opinions on social issues and may feel very close to each other.

On the surface, the emergence of heterogeneity has resulted in a rise of cultural awareness against a feeling of losing the society's core culture, and fuelled nationalistic issues up on the political agenda. But deeper and more important than that, *facing heterogeneity has paved the way for a new and permanent non-economic dimension of separation within the political arena*, namely the emergence of *conservative thinkers* versus the *contemporary thinkers*.

In simple terms, *conservative thinkers* are those who care about and differentiate people on cultural values and social attributes – like nationality, race, religion, and even gender. Most significantly, they *believe that the cultural values and social norms of the majority should dominate the society*, thus practically prefer a rather homogeneous society.

Contemporary thinkers, on the contrary, do not believe that the cultural values or social attributes mentioned above should differentiate people. They *do not believe that society should be dominated by any set of cultural or social values, but rather think of these values as private preferences or attributes on an individual basis*. Thus, they are open for and welcome a heterogeneous society. In that sense, they are the liberals on the cultural front.

THE NEW TWO DIMENSIONAL POLITICAL ARENA

As a result of these major game changers and their consequences, *the political arena now has two separate dimensions, one on economic issues and the other on (non-economic) cultural and social issues*.

And to complicate matters, *these two dimensions do not coincide with each other*. That is to say, the preferences of a voter in one dimension do not necessarily determine his preferences in the other.

In this two dimensional political arena, *either of the dimensions may naturally dominate the other from time to time, depending on the prevailing social, economic and political conditions, locally and globally -* and there is nothing wrong with that (as will be discussed in the next subsection). However, the trouble is that, as discussed before, sometimes the attention of the society is artificially and deliberately distracted towards non-economic issues by concentrated economic powers or populist politicians – and in a heterogeneous society with weakened Social Intellect, it is much easier to do so.

Whether the attention of the society is naturally diverted or artificially distracted away from economic issues, the end result is that the check-and-balance relation between politics and economics weakens or even disappears, and economic troubles may build up in the background without being cured for along time – eventually rising the risk of a system breakdown.

THE NEED FOR A RESTRUCTURING OF THE POLITICAL SYSTEM

When a second permanent dimension on cultural and social issues, which is independent of the economic dimension, appears on the political agenda, members of a society (as voters in the democratic system) may have several different combinations of preferences regarding these dimensions. Thus, proper representation of these preferences emerges to be a major problem in the political system – especially when there are only two or three outstanding political parties which can not cover even the most basic differences in preferences. Or, from another viewpoint, a larger set of different preferences necessitate a higher competition among political parties, which can not be realised in democratic systems based on a very few political parties.

From the viewpoint of the political parties, there are now many diverse sets of voters with significantly different preferences, such that each party now needs to cover more than one set of preferences to receive adequate political support – while none of the parties have such an experience. Consequently, almost all political parties face identity-crises within this new heterogeneous environment.

In short, the once clear-cut match between the voters and the political parties has largely disappeared now, as both sides are lost in the search for the other. Clearly, both the voters and the political parties, and thus the society, need to travel on another type of learning curve to re-design their political system.

And all these will be discussed in detail in Book Four of this series.

The Natural Emergence Of Significant Non-Economic Issues

Focusing attention and awareness is a matter of relative importance. However important some economic issues may be, there may still arise some other more significant non-economic issues that naturally dominate the political agenda.

For instance, the emergence of global political issues, like major changes in international alliances and relations, or inter-society tensions or threats, or the breakout of wars, or mass migration, or some natural disasters or epidemics etc. may rightfully and rationally divert attention away from economic issues.

However, although giving priority to such non-economic issues is rational, still, at times like this, even the most significant economic troubles may remain unattended for a long time, and continue to worsen in the background without being cured, with potential negative consequences in the long run.

3.4   The Shift Of Attention Away From Politics

The discussion in the previous section was on the cases of shifts of attention to non-economic issues within politics. There are also the cases where the society's attention shifts totally away from politics, which is worse – as it has no rationality but just potential negative consequences.

The Spread Of A Diversified Set Of Attention Distractors

As discussed in Book One of this series, if there were a society which had solved its major economic and political issues completely and successfully, attained an optimal welfare level with high average incomes within acceptable inequality, and thus has ample free time for fun, then it would have made perfect sense for its members to engage their attention heavily in entertainment activities, as these increase individuals' happiness tremendously. However, if a society still has many major economic and political issues to be solved, all with a potential to go worse if left untreated, then, first, spending too much time and material resources on entertainment activities is a waste of society's limited potential, and second, sparing too much attention to them practically becomes a distraction of attention from the major issues that need to be solved. Thus, *involvement in entertainment activities*, while a necessity for the happiness of the society for sure, and a very innocent one on the surface, *becomes a source of harm to the long-term welfare of the society when exaggerated under inappropriate conditions.*

Unfortunately, the advances in digital communication technologies facilitate the spread of all sorts of entertainment, including sports, fashion, music, movies, games, jokes, stories etc., all of which distract attention effectively away from economic, social and political issues.

As discussed in Book Two of this series, social awareness is the greatest obstacle to cheating, both in economics and politics. For that reason, the distraction of attention from economic, social and political issues to any sort of entertainment makes cheating much easier. In that regard, the developments in digital technologies that offer easily and freely accessible entertainment activities are very welcome by the Cheaters.

Consequently, they may happily promote the spread of such attention distractors.

The distraction of attention through the spread of entertainment activities may be a major negative side effect of innocent developments in technology, or a deliberate promotion of attention distractors by some concentrated interest groups in the economy and/or their cooperating politicians. But in any case, the over-distraction of society's attention away from even political issues is a root cause of a major fall in the Social Intellect of the society and thus a danger for the stability of the western social order.

The Potential Effects Of Digital Technologies

As discussed in Book One of this series, the exponential rise in computing power in the recent decades make it possible to follow every breath that every individual takes in the digital environment. When the digital footprint of each individual on different networks that reveals his personal background, preferences, tendencies and desires can be tracked and analysed in detail, it becomes possible to know the individual better than he knows himself. And then, utilising the help of artificial intelligence, it also becomes possible to create an imaginary (virtual) world that corresponds to *a heaven-on-earth designed on a personal basis* for the taste of each individual.

THE CREATION OF PERSONAL VIRTUAL WORLDS UTILISING ARTIFICIAL INTELLIGENCE

As discussed in Book Two of this series, the next revolutionary development in digital entertainment will be *virtual reality*, which is primarily a complete immersion of the individual to an imaginary world created for the tastes of the individual by the help of artificial intelligence. For that purpose, the already available sets of gizmos will be further developed, enabling the total isolation of the individual from his environment, and letting him to hear or see only the imaginary world created around him. As this imaginary world is tailor-made to maximise his pleasure, with the help of artificial intelligence that knows the individual better than he knows himself, the individual will feel like he is in a heaven on earth whenever he is submerged in this artificial world.

And the best attribute of virtual reality is that, in their personalised imaginary worlds, every individual will attain an endless artificial happiness and satisfaction simultaneously, as in these imaginary worlds -contrary to the real world- everyone can be a winner without a need for corresponding losers.

Staying in such an imaginary world for extended periods of time in a frequent fashion will weaken the ties of an individual with the realities of the world he is living in. Actually, his imaginary happiness and satisfaction will eventually replace his need and desire to attain such happiness or satisfaction in the real world. Consequently, his shift of attention from the real world to the virtual one will also shift his attention away from the political and thus economic matters -like any rise in inequality against him or the decrease in his wealth and welfare.

Therefore, virtual reality may become the ultimate attention distractor that will diminish an individual's motivation to stay aware of his economic and political environment, diluting his social awareness of the real world he is living in – again to the very pleasure of some concentrated interest groups in the economy and/or their cooperating politicians.

SOCIAL MEDIA – THE HIDDEN DANGER

The social media, another by-product of the advanced digital technologies, serves many purposes, some very suitable and beneficial in terms of communication capabilities. However, one of its dominant by-products is the widespread presentation of almost artificial super-humans (real people may be, but at the selected best of their times and conditions) living in extreme luxury and beautiful environments, followed by many who fail to realise that what they are witnessing is either extreme or just unreal. As these innocent followers of social media naively start to assume that these artificial lives they are witnessing on social media are actually how the-rest-of-the-others in the society live (i.e. the average rather than the extreme), they become overly unhappy with their own real lives. The hidden trouble is that, the gap between their own real lives and those presented to them is so huge that, many of them start feeling like they are doomed to stay in the miserable conditions they currently live in, without any hope of improvement. Consequently, from a political viewpoint, they may come to believe in the need for the destruction of the current social order without any opinion on what may come next. In other words, they may discredit the whole social order, rather than analysing and understanding it - which would have enabled them to see what is going wrong and how it could be cured without the total destruction of the social order, improving both their and the society's welfare. But rather than improving their Social Intellect and creating a political demand for rational improvements in both the economic and political systems, they may just lose their belief in the whole social order and become open to populist and/or extremist opinions that may eventually threaten the stability of the social order.

VIRTUAL REALITY VERSUS SOCIAL MEDIA

As discussed above, in social media, everybody seems to be perfect except the individual himself, which makes him feel weak, deficient and unhappy, and consequently, open to extremist political ideas threatening the stability of the social order.

On the contrary, in the imaginary world of virtual reality, the individual is perfect and better than everyone else at all times, living in the best imaginable world specifically designed for him by artificial intelligence, without facing any troubles, making him feel powerful, satisfied and happy. And, much less interested in real life economic and political issues – thus never threatening the stability of the social order even if there may be many troubles within the economic and political systems.

In that regard, the artificial happiness that will result from the potential rise and spread of virtual reality (enabled by the development of artificial intelligence), may eventually dominate the unhappiness caused by the social media, and help to create a more stable, happier but much less intellectual society.

Such a weakening of the Social Intellect of the society may practically introduce more stability to a social order becoming more and more obsolete against the major game changers arriving one after the other in the medium run, as it diverts attention away from economic and political issues. However, as the structural inadequacy of the underlying economic and political systems worsen in the long run, and consequently the overall welfare of the society fall way below its acceptable threshold, it will be incredibly difficult for the society to escape an eventual system breakdown – except that it will then have to handle the chaos with a much lower Social Intellect.

3.5   Intellectual Inequality

Section 3.2 investigated why, through the recent decades, even in the western societies, when inequality rises and/or growth rate falls too much, the check-and-balance relation between economics and politics fails to cure these troubles. The discussion in Sections 3.3 and 3.4 revealed that there are two fundamental reasons for this failure: the shift of attention to non-economic issues within politics and the shift of attention away from politics, *both of which are facilitated by the weakening of the Social Intellect of the society to inadequate levels*. Therefore, a closer look to the weakening of the Social Intellect of the society may further clarify the dynamics of this failure.

INTELLECTUAL INEQUALITY

In Book One of this series, the concepts of intellectually-adult and intellectually-childish were introduced. Being intellectually-adult is defined as being educated and experienced in social sciences that enables the individual to develop adequate awareness of the social environment around him, such that he can appropriately play his role as a political participant (at least as a voter) and as an economic participant (at least as a consumer and a supplier of labour) in the society, as implicitly assumed by the western social order based on Free Market Economy and Democracy. Or, in short, an intellectually-adult is an individual with adequate Social Intellect.

It directly follows that an intellectually-childish individual is one who fails to play his role appropriately in the western social order from time to time -if not always- as he has inadequate Social Intellect.

And the Social Intellect of an individual is not a stable attribute. It can be improved through education and experience to convert an intellectually-childish individual to an intellectually-adult. Or, it can be weakened either by the rising complexity of the environment due to the arrival of major game changers, or by the distraction of the individual's attention away from social issues, or both.

At any time, there are both intellectually-adults and intellectually-children in a society, with different proportions, and with all shades of grey in between. The overall Social Intellect of the society, therefore, is the average of the intellects of its members.

As the members of the society have different levels of Social Intellect, there is also the concept of *intellectual inequality*, regarding *the distribution of Social Intellect within the society* and the gap between those at the top versus those at the bottom.

And, just like the case in economics in Section 1.1, where the average-income-per-capita does not mean much without considering income inequality (i.e. the distribution of income), *in the case of Social Intellect, the average-social-intellect of the society does not mean much without considering intellectual inequality (i.e. the distribution of intellect)*.

THE HIDDEN TROUBLE

As discussed in section 2.3, when a major game changer arrives and the complexity of the environment rises, the average Social Intellect of the society weakens.

But, more important than that, *as the Social Intellect of a society weakens, not everybody loses Social Intellect at the same rate*. Some may keep their Social Intellect adequate while some others' intellect may weaken to inadequateness.

As discussed in the previous chapters, from the economic perspective, when the complexity of the environment rises and the welfare of the society falls, this fall mostly includes a rise in *income inequality*. The major trouble is that, even before the rise in complexity, most losers in the previously lower income inequality already had below average Social Intellect in practise. As income inequality rises with complexity, they now have to concentrate more on matters of economic survival, distracting their attention further away from sustaining their Social Intellect, consequently facing a significant fall. On the contrary, most winners in the previously lower income inequality already had above average Social Intellect in practise, and, as complexity rises, they mostly remain on the winning side of the rising income inequality, which enables them to keep their attention on sustaining their Social Intellect, or at least losing less of it.

Therefore, *following a rise in complexity*, not only the income inequality rises, but more important than that, *the intellectual inequality within the society rises* while the average Social Intellect of the society falls. Even worse, *most losers of rising income inequality are also on the losing side of the rising intellectual inequality*.

This simultaneous rise of intellectual inequality with income inequality is the real reason why the check-and-balance relation may fail to function properly for a long time -if not until a total system breakdown- under a Democracy.

WHAT IF INTELLECTUAL INEQUALITY IS NOT CURED

As discussed in Books One and Two, not all the intellectually-adults are goodwilled. Some become Cheaters, who will try to create concentrated powers in economics and politics, to serve their own interests at the expense of the society. These Cheaters prefer to have a society with inadequate social awareness, as such a society can easily be guided to vote against their own interest and serve the Cheaters' interests within the framework of a Democracy.

Consequently, following a game changer, the remaining Cheaters[25] will naturally prefer to preserve any weakness in the average Social Intellect of the society and the accompanying rise in intellectual-inequality, for their own benefit.

Once some individuals lose their social awareness too much and become intellectually-children, they may not even be aware of the intellectual inequality against them, and as a consequence, they may not develop much of an awareness of the rising income inequality against them either. And the winners of the income inequality are usually bright enough to enjoy their economic privileges behind closed doors to facilitate such unawareness. This way, the intellectually-childish losers will not even show any political reaction to demand an appropriate policy change[26].

As discussed in Section 3.4, in a dystopian future society, which is unfortunately not impossible, there may be a huge proportion of intellectually-children in the society, experiencing an imaginary happiness in their virtual-worlds or enjoying many sorts of free entertainment supplied for the masses, while simultaneously living under miserable economic, social and political conditions in the real world. In such a society, only a minority of intellectually-adults, including many Cheaters, will live in and enjoy real-life good conditions. And the worst of all, the social order of such a society may retain its stability for a long time, as the intellectually-children may never recover adequate awareness to show any political reaction - at least until it is too late to save the established social order.

3.6 The Failure and The Cure

Section 3.2 has raised the question why, through the recent decades, when inequality rises and/or growth rate falls too much, the check-and-balance relation between economics and politics fails to function as expected and cure the troubles. Sections 3.3 and 3.4 have analysed the two primary reasons for that, namely the shift of attention to non-economic issues within politics and the shift of attention away from politics, and discussed the sub-factors under those primary reasons.

Naturally, in many cases, more than one factor mentioned in Sections 3.3 and 3.4 emerge and/or exist simultaneously.

AN ILLUSTRATIVE CASE

A simplified real life case can be helpful to clarify the analysis in this chapter. For that purpose, consider the societies on the two coasts of the Atlantic Ocean.

From the middle of the 20th century, the society on the west coast, namely the United States, was experiencing high economic growth, with moderate inequality that was acceptable within its culture. It had an education system and a press both of which refused to consider any potential virtues of any other economic system apart from their own, and this belief was further strengthened by the fall of the Soviet Republics and their economic system by the end of the 20th century. At that stage, the society on the west coast have believed that they have optimised their own economic and political systems.

The societies on the east coast, namely the West European countries, had travelled on a different learning curve, such that they were experiencing low inequality -thanks to their stronger social security systems-, with moderate economic growth that was acceptable within their culture.

Therefore, by the second half of the 20th century, the societies on both sides of the Atlantic were somewhere past the midway on their learning curves towards their own optimal policies, and although they were still swinging between liberal and social policies, they were at least enjoying some more stability with respect to their previous decades. And this stability has misguided these societies to believe that everything will get ever better in time as they travel further on their current learning curves. Consequently their attention started to shift away from economic and political issues, towards the joys of life.

Unfortunately, while their attention shifted away, negative divergences from their expected path to optimal welfare have already started to emerge in the background. On the west coast, competition started to decrease as concentrations of economic power started to rise, further rising inequality. On the east coast, too much social security started to decrease -the fear of the future, and thus- the motivation of individuals to try harder and innovate, further decreasing economic growth.

To make matters worse, some very slow but significant game changers were also emerging in the background, requiring major structural changes in the economic and political systems of all these societies, thus necessitating a re-start of their travels on new learning curves. For instance, the decrease in the birth rates coupled with the increase in expected lifespans were causing a fast ageing of these societies which will definitely shake the foundations of their social orders in the long run. Unfortunately, the social awareness of these societies on such issues were minimal by then, as their attention were distracted elsewhere.

And then came the two major game changers (namely, technological advancements and globalisation), which -unlike the slow developing ageing issue- have changed so much so fast.

First, concentrations of economic power have skyrocketed on the West Coast, and surpassing any previous cases by far, started to harm the welfare of the society - in the way discussed in Book Two.

And the two coasts were more integrated than ever before thanks to the spread of globalisation, thus the ocean started to carry the troubles emerging on its west coast to the east coast, and the negative transmission peaked during the economic crisis of 2008.

As the Social Intellect on both coasts have significantly weakened in relative terms with respect to the new complexities introduced by these game changers, the troubles in the economies of these societies were consequently transmitted to their political environment, eventually directing their attention to politics again.

But their Social Intellect has already weakened too much, and as expected in light of our previous analysis, this sudden rise of major troubles under the conditions of inadequate Social Intellect have enabled and thus resulted in the rise of populist or extremist political parties in most of these societies. Again as expected, these populist parties have distracted the attention of the societies away from the underlying real economic issues to non-economic side issues like nationalism, while concentrations of political power have started to emerge on both coasts.

By the first half of the 21st century, the ongoing inadequacy of the Social Intellect of these societies are preventing them from developing a full awareness of the scale of the troubles in their economic and political systems. Consequently, as if these societies are not in enough of a mess already, they embrace further major game changers, like the development and spread of artificial intelligence, although they do not have the slightest clue on their potential consequences.

As the effects of the game changers of the recent past and the potential effects of some new game changers of the near future get aggregated, the complexity of these societies' economic and political environments will rise further, and consequently the relative Social Intellect of these societies will weaken further. This may eventually threaten the stability of their social order – before these societies can have a chance to re-start their walks on their new learning curves.

Therefore, *if these societies are willing to sustain their social order, for which they will need to embrace major structural changes in their economic and political systems, then they need to develop an awareness of the significance of the threat to their social order as a first step. This will then keep their attention on politics, however, focusing on politics can not achieve much by itself unless these societies then direct their attention to the underlying economic troubles within their social order. If they can digest the fact that some painful long-term remedies have to be implemented (including major structural changes in their economic and political systems), then they can start analysing the current situation rationally and start their travels on their new learning curves.* However, that would require a huge leap in the Social Intellect of the societies in a relative short period time, and although such a leap is possible, it is in no way guaranteed unless it is explicitly targeted – as discussed in Book One of this series.

And in the best case where a leap in the Social Intellect is achieved, these societies will still need a long time to cure their new troubles and walk on their new learning curves towards their new optimal policies.

THE CURE

As the discussion in this chapter revealed, the strange persistence of high economic inequality within a political system built on absolute equality, or in more general terms the failure of the check-and-balance relation between Free Market Economy and Democracy, can be a result of two fundamental reasons, namely the shift of attention to non-economic issues within politics or the shift of attention away from politics, both of which are in turn consequences of the weakening of the Social Intellect of the society to inadequate levels.

This observation also reveals the cure. *First the intellectual inequality within the society has to be decreased, through rising the Social Intellect and awareness of those who became (or already were) intellectually-children, so that the average Social Intellect of the society will rise to an adequate level. Then, the check-and-balance relation will naturally start to function again*, rising a political demand to cure the troubles in the economy whenever needed.

In short, although politics is not only on economics, and some real significant non-economic issues may arise from time to time and dominate the political agenda, the check-and-balance relation between politics and economics still remain to be valid in the background in the long run - as described throughout the previous chapters. As the temporarily weakened Social Intellect of the society re-rises, and any significant non-economic issues with higher priority are resolved, the economic issues will re-start to effect political choices.

In an adequately intellectual society living in a Democracy, the relation of economics and politics can not remain broken for too long.

CHAPTER 4
SOCIAL SECURITY

4.1 Taxation-and-Distribution

As discussed through the initial chapters, too high inequality both decreases the growth rate of the economy and threatens to bring social unrest which endangers the stability of the social order, and therefore has to be dealt with decisively.

One indispensable tool for dealing with too high inequality is *taxation-and-distribution* under various social security structures, whose main purpose is to decrease after-tax inequality whenever pre-tax inequality is too high.

THE NEED FOR SOCIETY SPECIFIC APPROACHES

Taxation-and-distribution structures have many varieties with significant differences in their principles and applications. To design the most feasible social security system for itself, a society first has to understand *why* it really needs to establish such a system, and then decide *how* to do it.

And the fine tuning of these structures requires the differentiation of taxation-and-distribution approaches for different age segments within the society, specifically for the young (those below working-age), for the elderly (those above working-age) and for the working-aged.

THE NEED FOR OPTIMISATION

Establishing taxation-and-distribution structures targeting each of these age groups is socially a great idea. However, structuring and applying taxation-and-distribution is tricky. If taxation-and-distribution is too weak, the negative consequences of too high inequality will remain even after taxation. If taxation-and-distribution is too strong, this time negative consequences of too low after-tax inequality will arise. Thus, there is a need for the optimisation of these structures for each age group, on a society basis.

4.2   Social Investment For The Young

The taxation-and-distribution structure regarding the young should primarily be considered as an economic and social *investment* for the society, as the young, namely those below their mid-twenties, are the future of the society.

What Social Investment For The Young Should Be

The young deserve to grow up under the best conditions, provided by their family whenever possible, and by the society if needed. But much more important than that, any adequately intellectual society, for its own sake, must make sure that the young grow up to become economically and socially contributing individuals, rather than becoming economic and social burdens on the society.

This requires the existence of at least four basic types of insurance, or direct financial aid, for the young: for education, for health, for nutrition, and for shelter. The society may require parents to buy such insurance for their children, or if that is not feasible for economic reasons, the society may supply such insurance for all the young free of charge. The economically-advanced western societies are supposed to have enough resources at least for the second option, if they realise that it should have the top priority within their overall taxation-and-distribution structures.

Moreover, as will be discussed further in Book Five of this series, fertility rates are decreasing in almost all the societies. It is therefore necessary to support families, not only with back up insurance, but rather with direct financial aid for the education, health coverage, nutrition and shelter of their children, in order to promote higher fertility rates.

Why Social Investment For The Young Is Needed

The need and cost for health, nutrition and shelter support are self-evident. The support for education, however, is more critical in principle and trickier in practise, while also being the costliest. It therefore requires a closer look.

To start with, education has two basic components: social education and professional education.

As discussed in Book One, *social education* is necessary for all the members of the society, in order to enable their developing adequate Social Intellect, which in turn will develop their social awareness and let them add value to, or at least do not inflict harm on, the economic system as consumers and the political system as voters. Thus, providing social education free of charge is a necessity for the society for the well-functioning of its social order based on Free Market Economy and Democracy, in a stable and sustainable fashion.

As discussed in Book Two, fair opportunity in having *professional education* (and employment), is the first condition for the establishment of Fair Competition in the economy, which in turn maximises the economic growth and the welfare of the society in the long run.

Looking closer, as discussed in Section 2.2, fair opportunity in having professional education (and employment) is required to make sure that those with the highest potential to succeed in a competition, and thus create the highest value for the society, should be able to join the competition. In other words, fair opportunity is required to have the optimal allocation of human resources in the economy. This, in practice, requires that each young member of the society is oriented in line with his individual abilities to receive a professional education in a field in which he can have a *comparative advantage*[27] over the others, thus be as successful as possible for himself and as valuable as possible for the society. It directly follows that, the more capable an individual, the more opportunity he has to be given at both professional education and employment, solely based on his personal capabilities, without any practical limitations.

Finally, having fair opportunity in professional education serves social justice from the viewpoint of each young member of the society - simply because, if things start to go wrong at the very beginning of someone's life, due to being born into a family that can not enable him to receive any professional education even if he has the necessary merit and capabilities, it is incredibly difficult to correct for such lack of education in the future.

Therefore, *spending for social education for all, and for fair opportunity in professional education for those who deserve it, are the best investments for the society for the long-run.* This is simply because *the social and economic benefits the society will get in the long run, will more than offset the costs of providing such social investment for the young in the short run.*

However, the above paragraph which seems to have a clear and innocent conclusion, actually contains tricky concepts that require a closer look.

Optimising The Costs Of Social Investment For The Young

Just like in any rational investment, the long-term benefits of supplying social investment for the young will offset the short-term costs, if and only if it is structured in such a way that, *only the costs required for the optimal human resource allocation in the future are born by the society.*

And optimal human resource allocation, which primarily concerns professional education, necessitates two conditions to be satisfied simultaneously.

The first condition is easier to guess from the discussions above: professional education of a young member of the society should be covered by social investment, if and only if he studies a field in which he has a comparative advantage over the others, thus will be creating the highest value for the society in the future. In other words, educating a young member of the society in a profession where he will not have a comparative advantage (due to his limited merit and capability in that particular profession) will be a waste of resources of the society. Thus, coverage of professional education need not and should not extend to all professions for all the young members of the society.

The second condition is that, covering the costs of a profession (even for those who have a comparative advantage in it) makes sense for the society only to the extent where the supply to be created by the social investment will match the demand for that profession in the future. In simple terms, if the demand for a particular profession will be a certain amount in the future, educating professionals that will create an excess supply for that profession with respect to the demand, will again be an unnecessary cost and a terrible misallocation of human resources for the society. This observation immediately reveals a further trouble: who will decide the future demand for particular professions and how. Making such planning is clearly not easy, but it is necessary in order to create a social investment system for the young with wide enough coverage but without unbearable costs for the society. Therefore, some state institution, preferably an independent one, has to be given this duty of forecasting demand for particular professions. Naturally, the forecasts will contain significant errors and safety margins have to be left for all professions. The professions that are not strategic or where the supply can be increased within a short time may have lower margins, while those that are strategic or require too long time to be supplied must have higher margins.

Unless social investment is limited by the forecasted future demand for each particular profession, the availability of unlimited coverage for professional education will sooner or later give birth to education institutions (including some universities) that offer low-quality education to those who do not have the necessary merit or capabilities to succeed in such professions in any way, just to profit from the free funding. In addition to wasting the society's resources, this approach will also harm the young being attracted to them. Such young members of the society will waste their time with such education, and worse, they will develop impossible-to-fulfil expectations of professional careers for themselves that will naturally never materialize – in turn creating a mass of unemployed people, unqualified in practise, but qualified only in their own minds and unhappy in their hearts, creating a potential source of social unrest for the long run.

In short, *supplying professional education for the young is a great investment for the future of the society, provided that it matches the highest-quality-education with the highest-merited young (considering their comparative advantages), in line with the forecasted or strategically planned demand for each profession in the future.*

The Trouble In Aging Societies

In a Democracy, the politicians serve the demands of the voters, and thus the eventual decision makers on the structure of taxation-and-distribution are the members of the society. This trivial observation creates a huge trouble when an aging society decides on whether the social investment for the young should be further strengthened or not.

Social investment for the young is a *great investment for the long run*, with *significant costs in the short run*. Consequently, such an investment makes sense for the beneficiaries who will be there for the long run. For instance, those who are currently at their working-ages but will be retired in the future, will benefit from a more productive and thus wealthier society in the future, as that society will be paying for their social security in the future. And, needless to say, the current young members of the society will benefit from being better educated, more productive and wealthier in the future. However, the current elderly members of the society, will not only fail to benefit from such investment for the long run for natural reasons, but worse, such an investment for the future will significantly dilute the resources that can be directed to their social security today. Therefore, such an investment is clearly against the interests of the elderly and will not be supported by them.

As the young are mostly below the voting age or are not even born yet, leaving them outside the current voter base, any decision to strengthen the social investment for the young needs to be supported by those at working-ages today, who still dominate the voter base in numbers. Under positive economic conditions, in which unemployment is low and incomes are relatively satisfactory, they can be expected to support the investment for the young. However, under negative economic conditions, in which unemployment may be high or job security may be low, and incomes are already strained, any further taxation for the social investment for the young may not be supported by the working-aged either.

Unfortunately, the situation in most western societies during the last couple of decades, and probably in the ones to come, resemble the second case. Decreasing fertility rates on the one hand, and increasing lifespans on the other, are creating fast ageing societies where the proportion of the elderly within the voter base is rising everyday. And, although unemployment rates seem to be low in most societies, the low economic growth rates do not present a shiny economic picture – making it harder to increase the tax burden on the working-aged for further investments for the young. Therefore, the societies are facing a situation where they are sacrificing the future of their young and of themselves, based on short-term economic considerations. As an unfortunate consequence, the social investment for the young will probably remain below optimal levels in the foreseeable future in most societies, and will continue to be a major obstacle to establishing Fair Competition.

4.3   Social Security For The Elderly

What Social Security For The Elderly Is, And What It Should Be

Any society is supposed to have some sort of social security for their elderly, to protect and care for them at the later stages of their life, when they are not supposed to be competitive in the labour market anymore and do not have a chance to go back to productive work to finance themselves.

Under the current applications in most societies, social security for the elderly is primarily made up of pension payments for those who have worked previously and retired. These pensions for the retired are variable-payment schemes, where the amount received usually depends on the working-age income and years worked on an individual basis. Conceptually, the closer the pension amount to the actual income of the individual during his working years, the stronger the social security - and vice versa. Needless to say, the stronger the pension schemes, the higher their burden on the taxpayers.

A weak pension scheme, while minimising the tax burden on the taxpayers, will not be enough for the elderly for a decent life above poverty limit. And worse, by definition, those who have not ever participated in the labour force (i.e. not worked or employed) have no pension benefits anyway. But the elderly are defenceless and uncompetitive, and leaving them to their own demise, for whatever reason, should not be acceptable in any civilised society.

Therefore, in addition to the current variable-payment pension schemes, in principle, a civilised society should offer some sort of *health insurance*, plus some *basic fixed-amount pension* in the form of a direct aid for shelter and nutrition, for all those beyond a certain age just for being senior citizens.

In practise, however, providing a basic income for all the elderly may create too high of a burden. Fortunately, from the viewpoint of social peace and justice, it is not a necessity. What is required is the compensation for only those with no other major income or wealth, and thus in need of financial support[28].

To sum up, this basic fixed-amount pension for those in-need, and the health insurance, and the variable-payment pension for those who earned the right to receive it, should together constitute the social security for the elderly.

Needless to repeat, as the strength of the total social security coverage for the elderly and the burden on the taxpayers are directly related, the total financial burden of the social security for the elderly must be contained within sustainable limits. But apart from sustainability, the strength of the social security coverage for the elderly has other economic consequences.

Need For Optimising Social Security For The Elderly

This subsection will discuss the consequences of too weak or too strong social security schemes, from the viewpoint of economic variables like consumption, savings, investments etc. Needless to say, the changes in these variables depend on very many factors. However, for the simplicity of the analysis, assume that all the other factors apart from the social security for the elderly are constant at moderate levels.

THE TROUBLE WITH TOO WEAK SOCIAL SECURITY FOR THE ELDERLY

Consider the common case of those who have participated in the labour markets during their working-ages, and eventually retired someday.

The trouble is that, no one knows how long a life they will need to finance after retirement. If there is adequate social security for the elderly, such that they can have a decent life based on social security benefits alone, this question is not that critical – as the society will support them as long as they live.

However, if the social security is too weak for the elderly, then they need to -at least partially- finance their older years themselves, through their own savings during their productive years.

Nobody knows whether they will live for just a few years or many decades after retirement. Consequently, any rational individual will try to protect himself for the most demanding case – namely a long life after retirement. This in turn means that, starting from his middle-ages he will save more and consume less till the end of his life, to protect himself from a miserable fate where he may face poverty at a time when he is not strong or healthy enough to go back to work anymore.

This over-saving of the middle-aged will probably not be offset by some over-spending of the young, as income mostly increases and wealth is mostly accumulated during and after the middle ages, and there is a practical limit on the consumption of the young based on borrowing. Therefore, in simple terms, when savings are high but consumption is low, on the one hand volume of investments will fall as the demand for consumption is low, while on the other hand the return on investments will fall as the supply of savings is high. Moreover, a too high proportion of the investments of the middle-aged and elderly may be allocated to non-productive ones, like housing and precious metals, which are believed to be less risky, but unfortunately economically less productive. Under these conditions, the society will face a lower-than-optimal economic growth.

It may be argued that, as has been happening in many eastern societies for decades, when savings are high but local consumption is low, savings may be channelled to other societies to earn higher returns. But this will fuel those other societies' economic growth and their consumption, and thus their happiness. Needless to say, it is difficult to define happiness through economic logic, however, it seems safe to assume that people are happier when they consume rather than when they save. Therefore, having accumulated wealth does not have much of a meaning if one can not consume some part of it during his own lifetime due to his fear of the future.

In short, *when social security for the elderly is too weak in a society, although the direct (and thus easily observable) costs on the budget and thus on the taxpayers are lower, the indirect costs in terms of sub-optimal -or much lower- economic growth actually dominate, and create a negative overall result. Moreover, conceptually, the happiness of the society will probably be lower, when they live in a constant fear of their future and consequently save too much of their lifetime earnings.*

THE TROUBLE WITH TOO STRONG SOCIAL SECURITY FOR THE ELDERLY

If social security for the elderly is too strong, then the opposite of what was described above will happen. Individuals will save less and consume more, as this time their risk is not living for too long, but living too short after retirement. They will enjoy life while they can, as their older years will be financially well supported by social security anyway. Therefore, this time savings will fall and consumption will rise too much. Investments will be needed, but can not be financed adequately or can only be financed at high interest rates – and in both cases economic growth will eventually fall below its potential, away from the optimal.

It may be possible to obtain financing from other societies, both for investments and consumption, and enjoy an overdose of happiness in the short run, but financing consumption or investments through external borrowing can not last forever. Sooner or later external financing will dry up, or its cost will rise too much, and the party will end.

Notice that the discussion above regarding a too strong social security for the elderly implicitly -but naively- assumed that such a social security approach can be sustainably financed by the society. And actually, many economically-advanced societies on the east coast of the Atlantic have once thought to be so, and strengthened their social security systems for the elderly beyond the limits that they can sustain in the long run. But as too strong social security decreases economic growth on the one hand, while societies are ageing beyond expectations on the other hand, their social security systems are fast becoming unsustainable, with a potential to create major social trouble when the fact becomes undeniable.

NEED FOR OPTIMISING SOCIAL SECURITY FOR THE ELDERLY

As the discussion in this sub-section reveals, *the strength and coverage of social security for the elderly must be optimised too – as both too weak or too strong systems are harmful for the economic growth of the society.*

The Trouble With Political Demand

Social security systems for all ages have to be eventually financed through the direct or indirect taxation of the employed labour at the working-ages, in this generation or in the coming generations. What is for sure is that, the elderly who have already passed beyond their working-ages will not be taxed in any way at any time (unless they are wealthy enough to pay taxes on their portfolio income, which is not the common case). But as societies age, with a lower number of young and working-aged people, and a higher number of the elderly, this taxation-and-distribution based approach gets more troublesome every passing day. Thus the social security entitlements, and primarily those for the elderly, have to be structured accordingly.

If a society has adequate economic power to sustain its current pension schemes and even add some basic fixed-amount pension for all those in-need beyond a certain age, it may and should go for it.

However, if a society already has an over-generous system with respect to its current economic power, it has no choice but to restructure its coverage, such that retirement ages will be higher and benefits will be lower. This drives most societies towards a politically difficult dilemma. On the one hand, it is socially very difficult and unfair to take back the promised entitlements to the current older generations, as they have no chance to go back in time and prepare themselves accordingly (through more savings in their working-ages etc.). On the other hand, the longer the system is kept unchanged, the higher is the risk of its total collapse.

Social security, like some of the rest of the state budget, is usually financed by borrowing, which -as will be explained in the coming sections- will eventually be paid back through the taxation of the future generations. However, there is a practical limit on borrowing, and thus the more a society borrows and spends today, the less it can borrow and spend in the future. Additionally, in aging societies, if the rising social security costs for the elderly are financed by the higher taxation of the currently shrinking labour base, economic growth will decrease significantly. Consequently, the costs of the larger older generation of tomorrow will have to be financed through the further taxation of the even smaller employed labour of tomorrow, within an almost stagnant economic environment. As there is a practical limit on how high a working-aged generation can be taxed, plus how much can be borrowed, the system will eventually collapse.

Therefore, there is a need for a dilution in the social security for the elderly in societies with currently over-generous systems. As mentioned above, any dilution in the compensations of the current elderly generation will be unfair, as they have no chance to go back in time and prepare themselves accordingly. Similarly, it will be unfair to dilute the potential compensation for the working-aged currently above their mid-fifties, as it is also too late for them to adjust their savings accordingly. However, the potential compensation for the working-aged currently between their mid-forties to mid-fifties can be diluted up to some extent, say by 20% in practise, as they still have a chance to revise their retirement plans and increase their savings accordingly. And the potential compensation for the working-aged currently below their mid-forties can be diluted further, say by 40% in practise, as they still have decades of work life before they reach retirement ages, and can re-adjust their retirement plans easily. Although this will mean some loss of benefits at their older ages for the currently working-aged, it is still much better than a total collapse of the social security system that will hurt everybody tremendously and may even endanger social peace.

The danger here is that, this *economic necessity* is not well understood by many voters who are currently in their working-ages, who tend to believe that they can keep intact the current over-generous system for themselves in case they *politically oppose* it. And they can not be blamed much either, as, on the one hand they lose Social Intellect through changing times and thus fail to see the economic facts by themselves, and on the other hand, they are not told the truth by the current politicians.

Therefore, the political decision - regarding social security for the elderly - in a democratic system, will be case dependent. Needless to say, the elderly will not support any decrease in their own entitlements in any way in any case. However, what the current working-aged voters will do may vary. Those at working-ages who realise that continuation of the current system for some more time will completely endanger their own entitlements in the future when the system collapses, may vote for some structural changes before it is too late. But those who fail to see this fact, may vote for the preservation of the current system – or even further strengthening of it.

And unfortunately, the situation in many societies (especially in those in Western Europe with over-generous systems where a restructuring is a necessity) are heavily tilted towards the second scenario, where the social security systems will be continued under their current structure until it becomes self-evident that they are about to collapse. And once at that stage, the initial reaction will probably be raising taxes on whoever is around. Unfortunately, that will not be a solution, as increasing taxation too much will decrease economic growth in return, and will become a self-defeating case. Consequently, sooner or later, these social security systems for the elderly will collapse, and then will be restructured from scratch, albeit after heavy financial losses and major social unease.

The Trouble With Economic Strength

The discussion in this section revealed that the social security systems for the elderly have to be optimised from two perspectives, economic and social.

From the social perspective, the optimal system should at least be enough for the elderly for a decent life above poverty limit, including those who have not ever participated in the labour force, to protect social peace.

From the economic perspective, the optimal system should not harm economic variables, and impair economic growth in particular.

However, a major potential trouble still exists: what if even the optimal system is not sustainable in the long run? In other words, what if even the optimal system requires too much taxation-and-distribution in a fast ageing society? Or, to be more precise, what if the economy is too weak to support even an optimal system?

These questions reveal the fact that *optimisation of the system is necessary but not enough for its sustainability. A strong economy, and thus high economic growth is another necessity, and that can not be achieved by taxation-and-distribution alone.* What the society definitely needs is Fair Competition to fuel economic growth, as will be discussed in Section 4.5.

4.4 Social Security For The Working-Aged

Competition, Winners And Losers

Whenever there is competition, there are winners and losers, and thus inequality. And decreasing inequality utilising taxation-and-distribution requires the taxation of the winners and the compensation of the losers. However, a closer look beyond that trivial observation, at who should be compensated up to what extent and who should be taxed up to what extent, will facilitate the discussion in the rest of this book. And that analysis can be made from the viewpoint of the *alternate paths to success and failure*, as discussed in Book Two of this series.

PATHS TO SUCCESS AND FAILURE

To remind briefly, there are four basic paths:

Merit is the combination of intelligence (or some special ability), professional education and experience, and hard work.

Excessive Risk Taking is undertaking irrational risks such that there is a low chance of ending up at success, and thus success may result if and only if good luck intervenes. Alternatively, it may be defined as taking risks where there may be a higher chance of success over failure, however, in case of failure the risk taker will be completely and irrecoverably ruined.

Luck is the unfair intervention of the randomness in the nature of the universe.

Notice that excessive risk taking and luck are considered separately, as being exposed to luck is inevitable, but taking excessive risks is a matter of choice.

And finally, *cheating* is pursuing unfair or unethical or even illegal competition, the ways of which are only limited by one's imagination.

From the viewpoint of these alternate paths, in principle, not all the losers deserve to be compensated heavily, and not all the winners deserve to be taxed heavily either. The practise, as usual, is more complicated.

THE COMPENSATION SIDE

The young and the elderly are by definition the economically defenceless members of the society, and in that regard, it is easy to accept that they deserve to be protected by the social security system. On the contrary, the ones at working ages are supposed to be able to financially survive by themselves. Unfortunately, many of them fail to do so, some for undeserved and therefore socially unacceptable reasons, and some for deserved and therefore socially acceptable reasons, as will be discussed next. However, compensation is required for all losers, albeit for different purposes – namely, *to serve social justice* and *to protect social peace*.

The Need To Serve Social Justice

Social justice requires that those losers who have not deserved their fate, have to be compensated as much as possible by the social security system.

These *undeserved losers*, primarily fall into two groups. The first group are those who have failed due to *bad luck*, although they have worked hard to succeed, without taking any excessive risks or cheating. The second group are those who were *not given a fair opportunity for education and employment*, and thus their motivation to work hard have not brought any success.

Moreover, sometimes macro-economic crises wipe out some businesses and jobs, and create unemployment, conceptually equivalent to some temporary bad luck. And worse, the ongoing trend in fast developing technology (from automation to artificial intelligence) may totally erase job opportunities for particular professions, and then, those employed in the disappearing professions have to be re-trained (re-educated) for another profession. This ever-more-common case is conceptually equivalent to a temporary loss of opportunity for employment. Both of these cases, even if they may be temporary, have to be compensated as much as possible by the social security system for the working-aged.

The Need To Protect Social Peace

There are also some losers who actually deserve their fate, and thus social justice does not require them to be compensated in any way.

These *deserved losers*, primarily fall into three groups. The first group are those who failed due to *lack of hard work* (i.e. lack of merit), even though they were given a fair opportunity for education and employment. The second group are those who have deliberately *taken excessive risks*, and ended up in failure naturally, without any need for any bad luck. And the third group are those who have *tried to cheat*, but somehow managed to end up in failure.

In principle, any compensation for those losers, is not only unnecessary from the viewpoint of social justice, but worse, will motivate others to behave that way if they know that in case of failure they will be saved by the social security system.

In practise, however, the situation is more complicated. When an individual becomes a loser, even for deserved reasons, if he simply accepts his fate and evaporates out of existence in silence, then indeed no compensation would have been required. In practise, unfortunately, when a loser has no hope left to gain anything back ever after, he will want to change the existing economic or even political system for any other where he may have a chance to start over. Such behaviour will endanger social peace and eventually threaten the stability of the existing social order, tremendously harming the welfare of the society in the process, and may even end up in a total system breakdown if the number of losers (deserved or undeserved) add up to significant numbers in time.

The society, therefore, has to realize that the social security for the working-aged has to compensate all the losers, including the deserved ones, above a certain minimum level, such that the losers will remain better off under the existing social order with respect to any other, and thus there will not be any widespread demand for a change in the economic or political system.

The Need For The Optimisation Of Compensation

As the discussion above reveals, on the one hand, the undeserved losers have to be compensated as much as possible for the sake of social justice. On the other hand, the deserved losers have to be compensated at the bare minimums to protect social peace but not to promote undesired behaviour like laziness, excessive risk taking or cheating.

And the final trouble is that, in practise, from the viewpoint of an objective compensation system, it is prohibitively difficult to distinguish between the deserved and the undeserved losers, as it impossible to measure luck, hard work, excessive risks or even detect cheating. In fact, more than one reason may exist in many cases. Consequently, the social security system has to treat all the losers equally and have a single compensation system covering all.

Merging the two facts above reveal that, the compensation system should neither be too weak (otherwise social justice will not be served at all) nor too strong (otherwise undesired behaviour will be promoted too much), and thus have to be somehow optimised.

THE TAXATION SIDE

When there is a need for compensation, there is a corresponding need for taxation. And on the taxation side, are the winners. And the discussion above should have already revealed that the winners can also be categorised into deserved winners and undeserved winners.

The *undeserved winners*, primarily fall into there groups. The first group are those who have primarily won on *good luck*. The second group are those who have taken *excessive risks*, but thanks to the extreme good luck on their side, ended up winning. And the third group are the *Cheaters,* as cheating is equivalent to artificially creating extreme good luck for oneself. As winning through either of these paths is unfair, social justice requires that those winners have to be taxed heavily.

The *deserved winners* are primarily those who have won on merit alone, without good luck, excessive risk taking or cheating. Naturally, they have to be taxed at the bare minimums, again to serve social justice.

The Need For The Optimisation Of Taxation

As the discussion above reveals, on the one hand, the undeserved winners have to be taxed as heavily as possible, while on the other hand, the deserved winners have to be taxed at the bare minimums, both for the sake of social justice.

This observation regarding the taxation of undeserved winners has strong consequences when these cases are distinguishable, as will be discussed in Chapter 5.

However, in most of the cases, it is prohibitively difficult to distinguish between the deserved and the undeserved winners, as it impossible to measure merit, luck, excessive risks or even detect cheating. In fact, more than one reason may exist in many cases. Consequently, in most cases -except the distinguishable ones-, the taxation system has to treat all the winners equally, and therefore, the taxation should neither be too heavy nor too light, and thus have to be somehow optimised as well.

NEED FOR THE OPTIMISATION OF THE OVERALL TAXATION-AND-DISTRIBUTION SYSTEM

The discussions in this subsection reveal that there is a need for optimisation on both the compensation and taxation sides. And, as will be discussed in the next chapter, even though compensation can be financed in various ways in the short run, *in the long run the compensation and taxation sides have to balance out each other*. Therefore, conceptually, the optimisation of taxation-and-distribution within the social security system for the working-aged has to be discussed as a whole.

The next question is then, whether the optimal social security system for the working-aged should tilt towards a stronger taxation-and-distribution or a weaker one.

Optimisation Of The Social Security System For The Working-Aged

FROM BEHIND THE VEIL OF IGNORANCE

In his book A Theory of Justice, American philosopher John Rawls, presents a thought experiment, where people should stay behind a *Veil of Ignorance* to appropriately decide the principles of justice.

To apply the experiment to our discussion and illustrate the relevant argument behind it, consider a simple case where an individual is given the choice between living in one of the two societies, where,

- society A has excessive inequality such that the winners win +500 and the losers lose -500,

and

- society B has moderate inequality such that the winners win +200 and the losers lose -200.

The catch is that, the individual has to make his choice without knowing whether he will end up as a winner or a loser in the society of his choice. If the individual knew whether he will be a winner or a loser before making his choice, naturally all winners will choose to live in society A and all losers in society B. The trouble arises when they have to make their choice before they know whether they will end up being a winner or a loser, thus behind a veil of ignorance.

Rawls argues that, in such a case, individuals will prefer to minimize their loss in the worst possibility, namely in ending up being a loser, rather than maximising their benefit in the best possibility, namely in ending up being a winner, and therefore, will choose to live in society B.

Applying this argument to the question of how strong should a social security system has to be, initially it can be said that, when societies think behind a veil of ignorance to reach a fair decision, they will prefer the minimization of inequality through heavy taxation-and-distribution.

The thought experiment, however, has a major implicit assumption, which weakens its final argument in our case: when the individuals in the experiment are making their choices, they assume that chances of ending up as a winner or a loser are equal and random, that is to say, totally out of their control. In practise, however, individuals have freedom to direct their lives as they choose to, and can tremendously improve their position for the better, and therefore this assumption does not hold, and thus the validity of the final argument weakens.

The argument, however, still points to a very strong and significant attribute of human nature, that *individuals' fear of failure is stronger than their desire for success*. And this is crucial for the conclusion of our discussion on *carrots and sticks*, coming next.

CARROTS AND STICKS

Any individual is naturally motivated to increase his income, and this behaviour is called *chasing the carrot* in the economics jargon. Similarly, he is also naturally motivated to avoid a decrease in his income, and this behaviour is called *avoiding the stick* in the jargon.

Assuming that, in general, the individual is bright enough not to take excessive risks, and ethical enough not to cheat (at least, not to cheat too much), what remains behind as the paths to success are luck and merit (primarily hard work). But luck is random and is out of the control of the individual. Therefore, what is left at hand is working harder to succeed. And in general, the harder he works the more his income increases – and vice versa. The critical question here is how his *motivation* (to try harder) changes as his income changes.

The concept of *marginal utility,* discussed in Section 1.3, plays a crucial role in answering this question. Remember that, because of the marginal utility of income, a unit change in income is *not* equivalent to the same amount of change in welfare of the individual at different income levels. When he has a low income, a unit change in income brings a significant change in his welfare, but when he has a high income, a unit change in income brings just a slight change in his welfare. This relation of *the diminishing returns in welfare versus increases in income*, is shown in Figure 4.4.A.

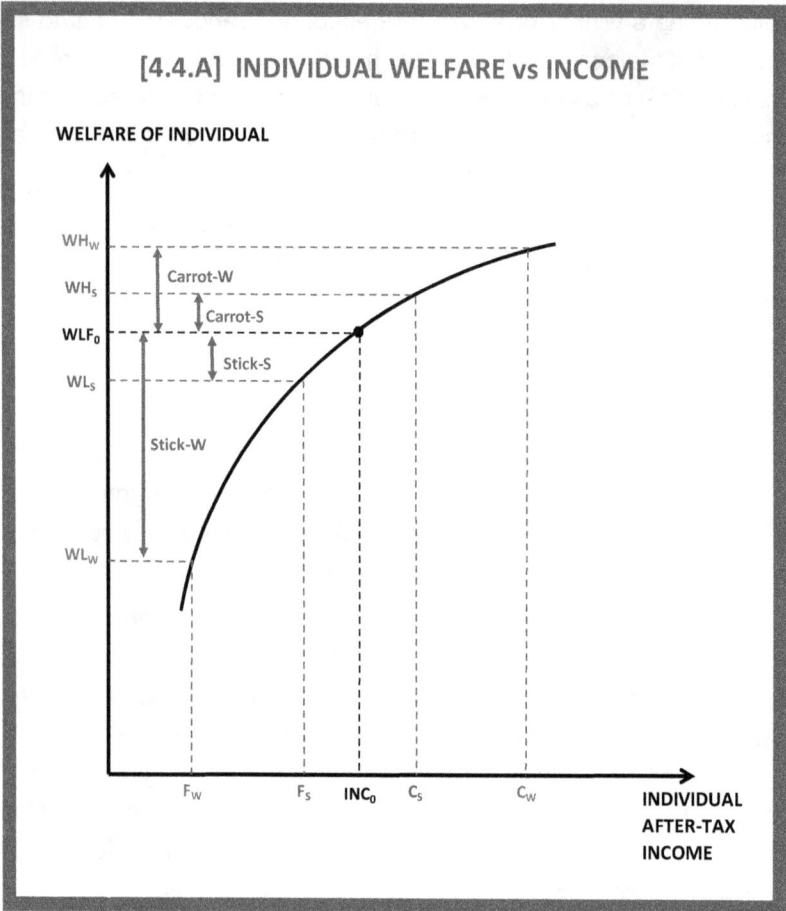

[4.4.A] INDIVIDUAL WELFARE vs INCOME

WELFARE OF INDIVIDUAL

WH_W
WH_S
Carrot-W
WLF_0
Carrot-S
Stick-S
WL_S
Stick-W
WL_W

F_W F_S INC_0 C_S C_W

INDIVIDUAL
AFTER-TAX
INCOME

Consider the situation of an individual whose income is shown by INC_0, with a corresponding welfare WLF_0 on the figure. Depending on his effort, his income and thus his welfare may change both ways, down or up. If he works harder and travels rightwards on the curve, his income will continuously rise, while a unit of gain (say $100) in his income will improve his welfare less and less. This is simply because, a $100 increase in income is more valuable for his welfare when his income is $1.000, but less valuable when his income becomes $3.000. However, if he starts to work less and thus travels leftwards on the curve, his income will continuously fall, and a unit of loss (say $100) in his income will worsen his welfare more and more. This is simply because, a $100 decrease in income is less harmful for his welfare when his income is $1.000, but more harmful when his income becomes $500. Therefore, increasing his income has diminishing returns, meaning that the more he wins the less that extra income will be worth to him, and losing his income has increasing returns, meaning that the more he loses the more that extra loss of income will hurt him. This asymmetry means that the individual will care more on not losing income than on earning more. In other words, he will care more about the stick than the carrot. Therefore, *the stick is a stronger motivator than the carrot.* This asymmetry has strong implications regarding the optimal strength of the social security system.

For the simplicity of the following analysis, visualise taxation-and-distribution as setting boundaries on the individuals' incomes, as taxation creates a cap for the winners, and compensation creates a floor for the losers.

When there is no social security, there is no floor or cap to the income an individual can attain in practise. But when social security is introduced, such that the winners (those at higher incomes) are taxed and the losers (those at lower incomes) are compensated, what the system effectively does is to limit the variation of after-tax incomes, such that there emerges a practical floor and cap for the income of the individual after the taxation-and-distribution.

And the stronger the taxation-and-distribution, the smaller the variation in after-tax incomes, and thus the higher the floor and the lower the cap. This practically corresponds to the weakening of both the carrot and the stick for the individuals.

In Figure 4.4.A the cases for two different strengths of taxation-and-distribution are shown, one weak (W) and the other strong (S).

F_W shows the floor and C_W shows the cap for the income of the individual (after taxation-and-distribution) for the *weak social security case.* For simplicity of analysis, the average of the cap and floor is taken to be the income level INC_0. The corresponding welfare levels are WL_W and WH_W.

Assume that when the individual works with average motivation, his income corresponds to INC_0. If he tries harder, his income can increase up to C_W, and he tries less, his income can fall down to F_W. Conceptually therefore, his *potential benefit from trying harder*, namely the carrot, corresponds to Carrot-W, and similarly, his *potential loss from trying less*, namely the stick, corresponds to Stick-W on the figure.

Now consider the *strong social security case*. F_S shows the floor and C_S shows the cap for the income of the individual (after taxation-and-distribution) for this case, and again the average of the cap and floor is taken to be the income level INC_0. Now the corresponding welfare levels are WL_S and WH_S, and the size of the carrot is Carrot-S and the size of the stick is Stick-S.

As seen on the figure, the weak social security system still enables a wide variation of incomes between F_W and C_W, but the strong social security system just lets a narrow variation between F_S and C_S. Consequently, the difference between the welfare levels is narrower in the stronger system.

Even without looking at the figure, it is easy to guess that, the narrower the variations get, the smaller will be the carrot and the stick. Indeed, as seen on the figure, both the carrot and the stick are smaller in the stronger system.

The critical observation here is that, because of the non-linear relationship between welfare and income, *when the strength of the taxation-and-distribution increases from the weak case towards the strong case*, -decreasing the difference between the floor and the cap, and decreasing inequality within the society-, the size of the carrot decreases a little, but the size of the stick decreases a lot. In other words, *when the taxation-and-distribution is made stronger, the stick weakens much more than the carrot*.

Remember the conclusion of the experiment made by Rawls, which states that an individual's fear of failure is stronger than his desire for success. What this means in practise is that, an individual's fear of the stick is stronger than his desire for the carrot. It directly follows that, when the taxation-and-distribution system is made stronger, consequently decreasing the carrot a little but decreasing the stick a lot, an individual's overall motivation will decrease significantly – and definitely much more than commonly assumed.

As explained in Section 1.2, when inequality falls too much, individuals will have less motivation to work hard. But now, this observation is taken one step further, as the fall in the motivation of the individual in this analysis is *not* just the result of the decreasing inequality, namely the decreasing gaps between the floors and the caps of each case, or the corresponding decrease of the gaps between the welfare levels in each case. More important than the decrease in inequality, the major decrease in the fear of failure (i.e. in the size of the stick) is the primary reason why the motivation of the individual will fall significantly – a conclusion revealed by the experiment of Rawls.

Coming back to the question at the end of the previous subsection, what this observation means in practise is that, when the strength of the taxation-and-distribution is increased, the fall in the individuals' motivation to try their best will be much worse than generally assumed and argued. Consequently, economic growth will fall first, and welfare will fall next. Therefore, although some social security system needs to exist for the working-aged, it is best to keep it at weaker levels of taxation-and-distribution, provided that it can still sustain social peace.

FINAL WORDS ON OPTIMISATION

Taxation-and-distribution can be utilised to decrease too high pre-tax inequality. And, as discussed in the previous chapters, inequality itself has to be optimised around moderate levels to maximise economic growth and welfare. Therefore, even if there were no sustainability issues, social security should still be optimised. A too strong or a too weak social security system will do more harm than good, just like a too low or too high inequality will hurt economic growth and welfare.

Keeping the need for optimisation in mind, it is every society's own duty to design a social security system in line with their own economic, political and social conditions.

A different structure that can be utilised by economically-advanced societies is discussed next.

What Social Security For The Working-Aged Is, And What It Should Be

THE CLASSIC APPROACH: TEMPORARY UNEMPLOYMENT COMPENSATION

Under the current applications in most societies, social security for the working-aged is primarily made up of some sort of *unemployment insurance*, that offers some temporary and partial income compensation for those who have recently lost their jobs without their own fault or will. The compensation is equivalent to some percentage of their latest income, paid for some temporary period after the involuntary loss of their jobs. The strength of the compensation increases as a higher percentage of the latest income is paid for a longer period.

Such compensation, by its nature, is just structured to be some sort of temporary financing for the individual until he lands on his next job. Therefore, its primary aim is not decreasing excessive inequality, or any inequality, as individuals with higher incomes receive higher payments and vice versa. In other words, it is not need-based. Therefore, from the viewpoint of having some taxation-and-distribution to decrease too high inequality for the working-aged, and thus to protect social peace, this approach does not serve the purpose.

In that regard, it is best to keep the strength of such unemployment insurance at the bare minimums, just to serve its own limited purpose, and in addition, implement a different structure for the aim of decreasing too high inequality and protecting social peace.

In the United States, the current unemployment insurance scheme is indeed at the bare minimums, or even less, as it is practically next to non-existent. Therefore, the structure described below can be and should be implemented in addition to the existing system of unemployment insurance.

On the east coast of the Atlantic, especially in some major economically-advanced West European societies, the situation is just the opposite. An overly-generous unemployment insurance already creates an unsustainable burden on the economy. Moreover, it demotivates individuals from trying harder, eventually having a negative effect on the economic growth in these societies. However, as the fall in motivation is a slow process, and motivation can not be measured explicitly, such a fall can stay undetected and unnoticed for a long time, while it steadily undermines the economic prospects of the society. Therefore, the current overly generous system has to be diluted as the first step, and only then, the structure described below can be and should be implemented in addition.

A NEW STRUCTURE: BASIC INCOME FOR THE UNEMPLOYED-IN-NEED

A new social security system for the working-aged that can be called *basic income for the unemployed-in-need* (shortly *basic income* in the rest of the discussion) can be structured, such that only the individuals at working-ages who simultaneously satisfy both of the conditions below can receive a direct compensation:

- he should be unemployed, for any reason including his own choice
- he should have no other income of any sort (rent, dividend, interest etc) and no other wealth (i.e. accumulated income) of any sort (cash, real estate, securities portfolio, bank account etc) above minimal levels

In other words, the individual will receive a basic income as long as he is unemployed *and* in need of financial support.

The condition of unemployment is mandatory, simply because, if the individual is employed, the direct compensation will mostly serve to subsidize the employer, rather than increasing the overall income of the individual, thus not decreasing inequality much. This is because of the fact that, if an individual would accept to work for a certain wage without such direct compensation, then when such compensation is introduced he will accept to work for a lower wage – as in the second case where there is compensation, his total income (with lower wage plus the compensation) will still be above his higher wage without the compensation[29]. Thus, the compensation will serve to decrease the wage paid to the individual, practically subsidising his employer.

The condition for financial need is also mandatory, simply because, the mere definiton of unemployed in this structure covers everybody in the society within the working-ages unless they are employed. In practise, most of these unemployed, many being voluntarily so, will not be in a financial need from the viewpoint of being on the margin of creating social unrest. Therefore, introducing the condition of financial need[30] significantly decreases the number of individuals who will be beneficiaries of this basic income, and consequently the burden of such distribution on the taxpayers.

Needless to explain, this structure will serve to decrease excessive inequality and protect social peace.

NEED FOR OPTIMISING SOCIAL SECURITY FOR THE WORKING-AGED, AGAIN

The previous discussions have revealed that, if the social security for the working-aged is too weak, it will neither result in a meaningful decrease in inequality, nor will serve social peace. And if it is too strong, it will decrease inequality too much, and consequently affect the behaviour of the labour force: those in the lower parts of the income ladder will notice the weakening of the stick (as they will be entitled to a basic income in case of a job loss), while those on the upper parts of the income ladder will notice the weakening of the carrot (as they will face a too high tax burden limiting their income). And all these will result in the demotivation of the labour force, consequently decreasing economic growth.

The basic income scheme described above, however, has another direct affect on the labour market. As no one who is eligible for the basic income will accept to work for too little a difference in income, but rather demand a meaningful difference to bother to work, the level of basic income practically sets a floor (way above its own level) for the minimum wage any individual will accept. When the basic income is optimised, such distortion will not be much, and thus may even be welcome. However, if the basic income is too high, the distortion will be severe, especially for the unqualified labour who are practically at the lowermost part of the income ladder, resulting in a misallocation of resources in the labour market, and consequently a decrease in economic growth.

Therefore, a need for optimisation is clear from any viewpoint.

SUSTAINABILITY ISSUES

As explained throughout this chapter, if the strength of the social security for the working-aged is exaggerated, its burden on the economy will sooner or later become unbearable. To put more precisely, the desired distribution will become unfinanceable through additional taxation, and the social security system will become unsustainable. And that is just another reason for optimisation.

However, just like in the case with the elderly, a major potential trouble still exists : what if even the optimal system is not sustainable in the long run? Or, to be more precise, what if the economy is too weak to support even an optimal system?

Once again, it is self evident that *the optimisation of the system is necessary but not enough for its sustainability. A strong economy, and thus high economic growth is another necessity, and that can not be achieved by taxation-and-distribution alone.* What the society definitely needs is Fair Competition to fuel economic growth, as will be discussed next.

4.5 Fair Competition And Social Security

The Need For Fair Competition For The Sustainability Of Social Security

As discussed in the initial chapters, too high inequality both decreases the growth rate of the economy and the welfare of the society, and threatens to bring social unrest which endangers the stability of the social order. As most societies discovered this fact long ago, they looked for ways of dealing with too high inequality. The most intellectual approach would have been analysing the causes (like widespread cheating and/or concentrations of power within the economy) and introducing the cure (namely Fair Competition) that would *prevent the rise of pre-tax inequality* towards excessive levels. However, such analysis and action require much Social Intellect, time and effort. An easier and faster alternative solution seemed to be trying to cure for too high inequality *after* it arises, namely by *decreasing after-tax inequality* through some taxation-and-distribution. Unfortunately, that is not a feasible solution by itself, at least in the long run.

Considering the social security for the working-aged, when pre-tax inequality is too high to start with, on the distribution side, the number of unemployed individuals to be compensated is too high, and consequently the total amount of compensation required is too high. On the taxation side, economic growth rate is low (i.e. growth is way below its full potential), and thus the total size of the economy relative to the total amount that needs to be financed through taxation is inadequate. Consequently, the burden of taxation on the employed individuals, and thus the tax rates, are too high. This demotivates the employed from working harder, as increasing their pre-tax income will only marginally change their after-tax income under too high tax rates, which makes any extra effort irrational. This will decrease economic growth further, increasing unemployment further, and consequently necessitating an ever higher amount of taxation-and-distribution. Then the ratio of the amount to be taxed-and-distributed to the total size of the economy will rise further. As this cycle feeds on itself and worsens over time, the social security system for the working-aged eventually collapses.

The crucial observation here is that, the reason behind the described collapse of the social security system for the working-aged is *not* that the social security structure is too generous to start with. Just on the contrary, even a structure that is minimised to cover only the very basic needs of the unemployed-in-need (such that social peace can survive) will eventually collapse when the pre-tax inequality is persistently too high – as the required amount of taxation-an-distribution will still be too high with respect to the total size of the economy.

A similar trouble exists for the social security for the elderly, simply because, when inequality is too high many of the retired individuals' own savings are inadequate to support their welfare after retirement. Consequently, the amount of compensation required to cover even for their minimal needs is too high with respect to the total size of the economy. And under those conditions, nobody will even remember the necessity of the social investment for the young.

Therefore, *even in cases where the social security for the working-aged, and for the elderly, and for the young, are kept at their optimal levels, if pre-tax inequality is persistently too high, it is practically very difficult -if not impossible- to sustain the social security system in the long run.*

NEED FOR FAIR COMPETITION

Reading backwards, the analysis above reveals that if Fair Competition is established and consequently pre-tax inequality can be kept within moderate boundaries, the situation will reverse – at least for the optimised social security structures.

To clarify briefly, starting with the social security for the working-aged, when pre-tax inequality remains within moderate boundaries, on the distribution side, unemployment is lower, and consequently the total amount of compensation required is lower. On the taxation side, economic growth rate is higher (i.e. close to its full potential), and the total size of the economy is much larger with respect to the total amount that needs to be financed through taxation. Consequently, the amount of tax to be paid per person is much lower, and tax rates are moderate and rational. This motivates the employed for working harder, as their after-tax income will now heavily reflect the rise in their pre-tax income, which makes any extra effort rational. And this will increase economic growth further, decreasing unemployment further, and consequently requiring an ever lower amount of taxation-and-distribution. Thus the ratio of the amount to be taxed-and-distributed to the total size of the economy will fall further. As this cycle also feeds on itself and gets better, the social security system for the working-aged will remain sustainable[31] – at least for the optimised social security structures.

A similar conclusion is valid for the social security for the elderly, as when inequality is kept moderate, many of the retired individuals' own savings will adequately support their welfare after retirement, and the number of those who are in need of further support through basic income will be minimal, keeping the amount of compensation required sustainably low with respect to the total size of the economy. And finally, under those conditions, the society may even remember the necessity of the social investment for the young, and can create the required structures described in Section 4.2.

Therefore, *if pre-tax inequality can be kept within moderate levels through establishing Fair Competition, then in cases where the social security for the working-aged, and for the elderly, and for the young, are kept at their optimal levels, it will practically be possible to sustain the social security system in the long run.*

IN CONCLUSION

Once pre-tax inequality reaches excessive levels and stays there for a long time, even the barely-adequate levels of taxation-and-distribution fine tuned for the optimisation of after-tax inequality within the society, can become a too heavy burden on the economy, and can not be sustained in the long run. Therefore, *taxation-and-distribution alone is not an adequate alternative for the lack of Fair Competition in an economy.* Consequently, only in case Fair Competition is established up to some extent and thus pre-tax inequality is somewhat contained, the burden of adequate taxation-and-distribution can become bearable and sustainable.

The bottom line is that, *in the long run, optimal social security* (for the working-aged and the elderly and the young) can not sustainably exist by itself without Fair Competition, but *can exist only as a complement to Fair Competition*.

Optimising Social Security Under Fair Competition To Maximise Economic Growth

The previous subsection revealed that establishment of Fair Competition -at least up to some extent in practise- enables the *sustainability* of an *optimised* social security system. Needless to say, even if there is Fair Competition, if the strength of the social security is exaggerated, it may still become unsustainable - and thus optimisation is essential from the viewpoint of sustainability.

However, even if sustainability of the social security system were not an issue, the social security system should still be optimised as its strength has a significant effect on *economic growth*. The analysis of this need for optimisation from the viewpoint of economic growth requires focusing on *allocation of resources* – a concept introduced in Book Two of this series.

Moreover, in addition to the considerations of social peace, strength of social security also has implications for *social justice* and thus the analysis of its optimisation should include that viewpoint as well. And for that purpose, some other concepts discussed in Book Two and briefly reminded in the previous section, namely the *paths to success* and *the deserved and undeserved winners and losers* need to be included in the analysis.

WINNERS AND LOSERS, DESERVED AND UNDESERVED

Taxation-and-distribution involves, on the one hand, those who will benefit from distribution, but on the other hand, those who will be taxed. And not all distribution and taxation are fair when taken on the basis of the individual, as both winners and losers have travelled through different paths to success or failure. For that reason, the concepts of deserved and undeserved winners and losers were discussed in the previous section. In light of that discussion, depending on the structure and strength of the social security system, the practical application may serve social justice, or may as well fall far away from it.

TAXATION-AND-DISTRIBUTION, FROM THE VIEWPOINT OF ALLOCATION OF RESOURCES

As discussed in Book Two of this series, optimal allocation of resources is required for the maximisation of economic growth. And taxation-and-distribution changes the allocation of resources within the economy. The critical question, therefore, is whether the allocation will be changed for the better or for the worse by taxation-and-distribution.

The analysis of winners and losers in Section 4.4, and their paths to success or failure, clarifies the answer. When undeserved winners are taxed and the undeserved losers are compensated, taxation-and-distribution practically results in a better allocation of resources. However, when deserved winners are taxed and the deserved losers are compensated, taxation-and-distribution practically worsens the allocation of resources. Unfortunately, taxation-and-distribution systems can not distinguish between the deserved and the undeserved sides, and thus can not differentiate between them in application. Consequently, the cumulative net effect of taxation-and-distribution depends on whether the deserved or the undeserved sides dominate the economy *before* taxation-and-distribution.

Consider the case where conditions for Fair Competition are either not established or are being violated, thus the undeserved winners and undeserved losers dominate the economic environment. When taxation-and-distribution is applied in this case, it will result in a better allocation of resources. However, if Fair Competition is established, and thus there are only a few undeserved winners and undeserved losers, and thus the deserved winners and deserved losers dominate the economy, then taxation-and-distribution will result in a worse allocation of resources. As explained before, taxation-and-distribution may still be applied for reasons of social peace, however, its negative effect on the economy must be kept in mind.

IMPLICATIONS ON GROWTH

As discussed in Section 1.2, changes in inequality result in changes in the motivation of the working-aged, which in turn change the economic growth rate. If inequality diverges from its optimal (moderate) level towards either too high or too low levels, falling motivation will decrease economic growth rate.

And as discussed in Section 2.2, changes in allocation of resources also change the economic growth rate. A better allocation will increase the growth rate, and vice versa. And allocation of resources depends on the existence of both Fair Competition and taxation-and-distribution.

Integrating these observations will help to analyse how changes in taxation-and-distribution will change the economic growth rate under different conditions.

If conditions of Fair Competition are violated or do not exist, and there is too high inequality, introducing or strengthening taxation-and-distribution will cause two changes simultaneously. First, it will help to decrease inequality from a too high level towards the optimal level, and thus will increase the motivation of the working-aged, which in turn will support growth. Second, as undeserved winners and losers dominate the economy initially, it will improve the allocation of resources, which in turn will also support growth. The net effect of taxation-and-distribution at this stage will therefore be an increase in economic growth.

When inequality approaches optimal levels, the strength of taxation-and-distribution must be decreased and optimised accordingly. Otherwise, even if it helps to maintain a better allocation of resources, the negative effect of further decreasing inequality away from its optimal level (towards too low levels) will dominate, and the net effect on growth will eventually turn negative – even if the social security system can be sustained for longer.

If Fair Competition is established -at least up to some extent- in the meantime, then when inequality approaches optimal levels, the strength of taxation-and-distribution must be further decreased for optimisation. This is due to the fact that, when Fair Competition is established, the undeserved winners and losers decrease in proportion, and deserved winners and losers become dominant in the economy. In that case, the application of taxation-and-distribution will practically worsen the allocation of resources. Therefore, unless taxation-and-distribution is minimised, the negative effect of worsening allocation of resources, coupled with the negative effect of further decreasing inequality away from its optimal level, will be combined to create a significant negative net effect on growth[32].

In short, *when there is Fair Competition, the optimal level of taxation-and-distribution at moderate levels of inequality is closer to bare minimums, and therefore must be adjusted accordingly.*

The Unfortunate Case Of Good Luck For The Society

An unfortunate case for a society is a period when high growth is achieved due to overly-positive external conditions (mostly beyond its control, primarily resulting from good luck), while having a strong taxation-and-distribution system in place. A natural reaction under such cases is further strengthening the social security system, naively believing that such conditions will last forever and the stronger system will remain sustainable. And when the natural reaction comes out to be just the opposite of the rational reaction, the price for this misunderstanding is paid in the long run, in the form of a lower economic growth first and a collapsing social security system next.

An example of such optimistic behaviour is the case of many societies on the east coast of the Atlantic, who have experienced a set of very positive external conditions after the Second World War, and strengthened their social security systems aiming to become higher-welfare societies. However, their overly-strong social security systems have silently decreased the motivation of their workforce and negatively effected their economic growth. As external conditions deteriorate, and simultaneously their societies age due to longer life-spans and lower fertility, the sustainability of their systems are now in question.

The Trouble With Politics

Politicians need the support of their voter base in order to come to power and to stay there afterwards. This simple fact, unfortunately, causes major trouble in both the establishment of Fair Competition and the optimisation of taxation-and-distribution.

The trouble arises from the fact that, *while social security is easily observable by the society* – as all can see the benefits reaching their pockets, *Fair Competition is not so easily observable*, as it has a significant but implicit effect on the welfare of the society.

The situation is worsened by the fact that *a stronger social security system can be financed through borrowing in the short to medium run, thus its burden on the taxpayers may stay the same in the meantime, and thus there will not be many opponents to strengthening the system.* In other words, *the social security system becomes a borrow-and-distribute system in the shorter run, before it inevitably converts to some taxation-and-distribution system in the longer run.*

This makes social security a great tool for politicians, especially in two cases. First, when there is too high inequality in the society and thus most voters are looking for a relief[33]. And second, when the economy is strong due to temporary internal or external conditions, and thus it can handle more borrowing and distribution in the short run. In both cases, the social security system may be strengthened way beyond its optimal level and/or kept there for too long, to gain political support. And such political behaviour mostly serves its purpose, as the society naïvely approves the efforts to create higher-welfare.

This mis-behaviour of the politicians and their voters, which is mostly carried out with good intentions, is further supported by the practical fact that, establishing Fair Competition (instead of strengthening social security) is a much more difficult and time consuming approach.

Unfortunately, all this somewhat innocent behaviour, can sometimes find other supporters who are *not* that goodwilled. When concentrated economic powers emerge in the markets at the absence of Fair Competition, they may consider that strengthening social security through borrowing-and-distribution will not hurt them, but just on the contrary may even enlarge their customer base further, while it will satisfy the needs of the society financially and emotionally for some time, leaving them enough space and time to further concentrate their economic power. Naturally, these concentrated economic powers support the strengthening of social security through borrowing by the state, rather than establishing or strengthening Fair Competition, both to decrease any potential political reaction of the masses and to serve their own economic interests. Even though economic growth stays below its full potential as a result of too much social security and too little Fair Competition, and eventually the social security system collapses in the long run, the price for such mis-applied policies will still be paid by the whole society, leaving the accumulated benefits of the concentrated economic powers in the meantime mostly intact.

In short, *in a Democracy, any society with inadequate Social Intellect will get more social security but much less Fair Competition, while the right approach for maximising the economic growth and welfare of the society in the long run is just the opposite.*

To re-emphasize, *a society with adequate Social Intellect, primarily establishes Fair Competition to naturally sustain inequality within moderate and acceptable levels, and further support the system with social security to take care of any residual or temporary fluctuations.*

Failure In Serving Social Justice

Before completing the analysis on social security and Fair Competition, it is crucial to mention that, even if the basic income for the unemployed-in-need scheme proposed in Section 4.4 is established within the social security system, it only serves to keep social peace, but not to attain social justice, as the undeserved losers are not necessarily unemployed.

There are at least two sets of hidden undeserved losers in an economy without Fair Competition. First, many people who were not given a fair opportunity to education or employment may still be employed, but at much less qualified professions or positions than their merit justifies and they deserve. And second, as discussed in Book Two of this series, when there are concentrated powers in the economy who happen to be on the demand side of the labour market, those on the supply side, namely the employed, may have no choice but to accept much lower packages (lower wages and less side benefits) with respect to what their merit deserves, and thus with respect to what they could have got under conditions of Fair Competition.

And once social justice is betrayed for the working-aged through the failure of establishing Fair Competition in the economy, the unfairness continues to exist for the elderly as well, as the elderly were once at working-ages when they failed to earn and save as much as their merit justified. Therefore, if the elderly have not worked in an environment of Fair Competition during their own working-ages, even if the basic pension for the elderly-in-need scheme proposed in Section 4.3 is established within the social security system, it only serves to keep social peace, but not to attain social justice.

In short, *the establishment of Fair Competition is the only remedy for the failure of social justice, and therefore it can not be replaced by social security in this regard either.*

A Final Blow To Democracy

In Chapter 3, two major reasons were mentioned as the obstacles to the optimisation of inequality and establishment of Fair Competition: the distraction of attention away from the economic issues within politics, and the total distraction of attention away from politics.

Unfortunately, *a too strong social security system, especially when financed through borrowing rather than taxation, serves to amplify such distraction of attention that cripples Democracy. When individuals naively believe that there is a perpetual strong social security system that will protect them against the worst, during their working-ages and when they get older, they may lose some interest in economics and politics.* As discussed in Chapter 3, such distraction is easier than ever before under the current conditions in almost all societies, magnifying the danger.

Therefore, *optimising the social security system is not only a necessity for the well functioning of the economy, but is also vital for the well functioning of Democracy.*

And needless to say, *establishing Fair Competition* does not distract attention away from economics or politics. Just on the contrary, it *promotes competition* and consequently *motivates people to keep their social awareness on economic and political matters.*

For the well functioning of Democracy, therefore, a society with adequate Social Intellect primarily establishes Fair Competition and utilizes an optimised social security system as a complement to Fair Competition.

CHAPTER 5

RESTRUCTURING TAXATION FOR MAXIMISING ECONOMIC GROWTH AND WELFARE

5.1   The State Budget

Components Of Budget Spending

Most societies, at least those advanced enough to have a social security system, have three components of state spending, that are distinct in principle, but merged within a single state budget in practise: one for the *operations of the state*[34], one for the *social investment for the young*, and one for the *social security for the working-aged and the elderly*.

When the state budget is not explicitly separated into these components, the implicit allocation of spending among these components escapes the attention of the public. Though several detailed analyses are made on the state budget by the analysts, in practise such analyses just remain as expert-level-thought-exercises among the economists themselves, never impacting the economic and political decision making process of the society.

However, *if the components of the state spending mentioned above are clearly separated and reported by the state, it will enable much better economic and political decision making by the society, and thus a much better allocation of resources* – which in turn will increase economic growth in the long run. Therefore, any society with adequate Social Intellect should demand the separate explicit reporting of these three major components of state spending, to start with.

Need For An Intellectual Discussion Of The State Budget

Whenever the State makes a spending, it benefits somebody in the society. The beneficiaries may vary from a small concentrated group, all the way to the whole society. But in any case, the more the spending the more somebody will benefit.

And every bit of spending the State makes has to be financed somehow. Although there seems to be different ways of financing (as will be discussed in the rest of this chapter), in practise all will correspond to some sort of taxation of somebody sooner or later.

To be more precise, when some component (or sub-component) of state budget spending is increased, either some form of financing (taxation or borrowing) has to increase, or some other component (or sub-component) of the state spending has to decrease, or both have to happen simultaneously. Consequently, any kind of taxation and/or decreased spending on one side, with the corresponding increased spending on the other side, is actually a transfer of resources (and thus wealth) within the society from the tax-paying and/or benefit losing side, to the beneficiary side.

Social Intellect and awareness require that any kind of analysis regarding the state budget should consider both of these sides simultaneously, while this is conveniently forgotten in almost all economic and political discussions in the current practise, in all societies.

In principle, however, *any issue regarding any changes in the state budget, must answer three questions:*

- *Who will benefit from the proposed change in the budget,*
- *Who will pay for those benefits,*
- *Why this change and the resulting re-allocation of resources will increase the overall welfare of the society.*

Therefore, an adequately intellectual society should expect that,

- any interest group who demands to get some benefit through some further allocation of spending within the state budget, or

- any politician who promises some benefit to any interest group (from smallest to largest) through some further allocation of spending within the state budget,

should also answer the second and third questions above.

Otherwise, infinite irrational demands and infinite irrational promises to cover those demands will fly in the air without any practical consequence, or worse, with significant harm to the welfare of some or all of the society in case they are realised.

On the contrary, *when such demands or promises are discussed together with their corresponding sources of financing, thus clarifying the payers in addition to the beneficiaries, there will be a natural opposition to every change, and then there may be a real chance to discuss the potential benefits or harms of each change on a society-wide basis.*

Needless to say, no society will or can discuss the details of the state budget, but what is meant here is discussing the macro conceptual changes regarding the major components of state spending and the major sources of financing. Although they may not match each other explicitly, there still has to be a balancing in between.

In conclusion, the structure of the financing of the state budget, and the allocation of spending from the budget, are the heart and soul of political and economic policies. Two relevant spending components, namely the social investment for the young and the social security for the working-aged and the elderly, were discussed in Chapter 4. The financing side will be discussed in the rest of this chapter.

5.2   Taxation As The Primary Source Of Financing

Types Of Taxation

The financing of all the components of the state budget can be done in three different ways of taxation in principle, and these are almost always used together in practise.

- *Direct taxes*, such as the common income and consumption taxes for the individuals, and corporate taxes,
- *Indirect taxes*, such as the Central Bank's printing money,
- *Taxes on future generations*, such as financing of the budget through long-term borrowing by the state.

Direct Taxes

Direct taxes are the well known ones in practise, and there does not seem to be any need to discuss their current structure.

However, it is crucial to emphasize that, *the reason for direct taxation should not only be the financing of the state budget, but should also include the prevention of the over-concentration of economic power that may eventually turn into or support concentrated political power* – as discussed in Book Two of this series. Unfortunately, this second reason is not well recognized by the society although it has a significant effect on the well-functioning of the western social order in the long run. Consequently, the necessary structural modifications regarding direct taxation are missing in practise. These necessary modifications will be discussed in Section 5.3.

Indirect Taxes And Central Banks (1) : Consumer Price Inflation And Currency Depreciation

Following the end of the Bretton Woods system -which has tied the creation of money to gold reserves which can not be produced at will-, the Central Banks started to enjoy the luxury of printing money as they desire. However, *a Central Bank's freely printing money through any means at any time is actually a taxation in disguise, both on the income and on the wealth, of both the individuals and the corporations utilising that currency.*

And exactly for that reason, within the scope of their mission definition, which states that Central Banks should aim to contain consumer price inflation within certain limited boundaries utilising all the tools that have, Central Banks should care about the amount of money printed in the first place.

In the most innocent practise, when money is printed at a rate more or less in line with the real growth rate of the economy, such printing will not cause much of an inflation or currency depreciation, and therefore will only correspond to a negligible taxation, while some minimal level of inflation is good for many other reasons regarding the proper functioning of markets and economy.

However, *printing too much money will cause a combination of high inflation and/or currency depreciation, and therefore a decrease in the purchasing power* (called a *decrease in the real value of money* in the economics jargon), *practically equivalent to taxation.*

THE TROUBLE WITH FAIRNESS

When a Central Bank prints too much money, the ones who are taxed, individual or corporate, do not face a fair taxation, as such taxation is not rule based, but rather depends on how much one can or can not protect his/its income and wealth against inflation or currency depreciation. And, in practise, the higher the accumulated wealth, the easier to protect it against inflation or currency depreciation. Therefore, *the major burden of such indirect taxation does not primarily fall on the economic elite or on the major corporations, but rather on the rest of the society.* And when the amount of printed money gets excessive, this unfairness skyrockets.

Consequently, both for the sake of fairness, and to stick to its mission statement, a Central Bank is supposed to limit money printing within the practical boundaries set by the real growth of the economy. However, at many times and under many conditions, it may choose to act differently.

The analysis of the reasons for such change of behaviour is beyond the scope of the current discussion, thus the focus in this section will be on what happens when a Central Bank prints money beyond the limits justified by the growth of the economy.

AT REGULAR TIMES

In the classic approach, a Central Bank can print money (way beyond required by economic growth) and buy state debt (Treasury Bonds) with it, practically lending money to the state, hiding behind the argument that the state will pay it back someday in the future. The state in turn can allocate the new money in the way it wishes, and even though some may be used for social security purposes, much will be allocated to the operational budget for spending and investment in practise, at the discretion of the politicians running the state. Therefore, even during regular economic conditions, a process of indirect taxation, that mostly goes unnoticed by the society, is continuously at work.

AT TIMES OF THUNDER

And once in a while comes a thunder to make matters even worse. At times of crisis, like the last one in 2008, a Central Bank may have to print money in extreme amounts. When the Central Bank prints such amounts of money within a short time, and thus makes that money less valuable, it practically taxes every individual or corporation who has any income or savings in that currency, albeit at different rates based on their ability to protect themselves, as explained above. And when the Central Bank buys bonds or equivalent debt instruments with the newly printed money, coupled with the promise that it will have them paid back in the future, it practically distributes the proceeds of the indirect taxation to the issuers of such debt. If government debt is bought, this corresponds to a redistribution to the state. If corporate or private debt is directly bought, it becomes a redistribution to the indebted corporations or individuals.

In principle, the newly printed money distributed this way will later be taken back through making the indebted state or corporations or individuals payback their debt, and consequently, as the money in circulation decreases, the taxes initially collected from the society in disguise will effectively be refunded. Thus, the whole process will be reversed and neutralized. The practise, however, rarely fits the principle, if ever.

One trouble with this process is that, the ones who were taxed during the money printing process, and the ones who are refunded during the payback process -if ever- are usually not the same ones.

To make matters worse, the way this cycle mostly works in practise is that, first the state undertakes the debts of the corporations or banks because they are too big to fail, or the individuals because they are too many to sacrifice politically, and then the Central Bank buys out the debt of the state. The trouble is that, in most cases, these corporations or individuals will never recover enough to pay back their debt. So, if any payback to the Central Bank will ever occur, it will only be the state paying back its debts. And the state can only do so by taxing those individuals and corporations who managed to survive the thunder simply because their choices were rational and prudent *before* the thunder. Unfortunately, these individuals and corporations are mostly the ones who were indirectly taxed through printing money in the first place, as they happened to keep their income and savings through the thunder. Therefore, even if the process is reversed and the indirect taxes initially paid by those survivors of the thunder will practically be paid back to them, this will only happen through directly taxing them. Thus, the survivors of the thunder will be indirectly taxed first, and then directly taxed afterwards to compensate for the initial indirect tax on them. Therefore, *for the survivors of the thunder, who happen to be the prudent players in the economy, there is no escape from paying for the sins of the others.*

To make matters even worse, many of the corporations or individuals who were indebted beyond any hope of recovery when the thunder hit, were in that situation because they took excessive risks *before* the thunder, partially betting on the state to come to their rescue in case of a thunder, as a typical case of *moral hazard* - as discussed in detail in Book Two of this series. Consequently, when the state actually saves them as expected, it inescapably gives the signal that it will continue to behave that way in the future as well, promoting further moral hazard and excessive risk taking for the future, rather than promoting rational and prudent behaviour. Therefore, *such indirect taxation and redistribution is not only unfair for the survivors of the recent thunder, but is also harmful for the welfare of the society in the long run*, as it continues to generate the wrong signal for the next thunder.

A WAKE-UP CALL FOR THE SOCIETY

Printing money in line with economic growth serves certain practical purposes, thus can be acceptable up to some extent. However, printing money at a pace above that required by economic expansion will mean an unfair indirect taxation on some, coupled with a potentially unfair distribution to others. Such an unfair redistribution of wealth from some to others clearly violates the requirement for optimal allocation of resources for the maximisation of the welfare of the society, and therefore should not become a common practise at regular times.

At times of thunder, it may really be required to push the limits, at least to save some strategically indispensable sectors like finance and insurance, but in such cases, the distribution process, which is eventually handled by the state, has to be carried out in a transparent and politically endorsed way, and by keeping the short-term and long-term interests of the society above all. For instance, instead of buying corporate debt, the state may prefer to inject capital and become a shareholder itself – just to sell back the shares once the thunder is over, to recover its initial contribution fairly and adequately. *Unfortunately, especially at times of thunder, transparency disappears, and the best interest of the society is usually sacrificed under the influence of some groups with concentrated economic interests.* Needless to say, there is no cure for this unfair taxation and distribution process unless the society develops adequate Social Intellect and demands further accountability from its political agents.

THE LUXURY OF HAVING A RESERVE CURRENCY OR ISSUING SAFE HEAVEN ASSETS

If a Central Bank is the issuer of a so-called *reserve currency*, namely a currency that is widely trusted, used and held worldwide, that Central Bank can enjoy this status when printing money, as it has the ability to tax everybody who happens to have some savings or income in that currency, wherever they may be in the world, independent of whether they are citizens (of the society of the reserve currency) or members of other societies. However, that Central Bank will naturally finance only its own state with the newly printed money, which in turn will buy out only the debts of its own citizens, corporations and banks. So, *for the Central Bank of the reserve currency, the indirect taxation through printing money* and creating currency depreciation, practically *means taxing many members of other societies, while distributing the benefits solely to its own society.* Therefore, such printing of reserve currency is beneficial for its own society.

By the same token, if that Central Bank wants to reverse and neutralize that process later on, its own state, as the primary debtor paying back its debt, will have to tax its own citizens. So, *the reversal of the process will practically mean paying back the indirect taxes paid by many members of other societies, through directly taxing only their own citizens.* Therefore, that Central Bank will only reverse the process if the domestic troubles created by the process (like a high local inflation) out-weight the benefits, or it becomes too clear that the currency may soon lose its reserve status unless the process is reversed up to some extent. Otherwise, the members of the other societies should be ready to wait for a very long time for such reversals, as such reversals will probably happen just before the end of the universe.

In short, a Central Bank with a reserve currency may be given somewhat more freedom in printing money by its own society (provided that it does not push too far and lose reserve currency status), as it happens to indirectly tax the members of other societies as well, while all the benefit of the distribution remains within its own society. By the same token, if someone is a member of any other society without a reserve currency of its own, and holds a reserve currency for whatever reason, he should be aware that he may become subject to indirect taxation by the Central Bank of this reserve currency.

Similarly, if a society has the ability to issue *safe heaven assets,* like government bonds that are trusted and invested in by other societies, it can tax the investors of these other societies in several ways. For instance, it can tax them directly and explicitly through having some withholding tax on interest payments received by foreigners. But worse, it can tax them indirectly by restructuring payment terms and bond maturities anytime and anyway it may want to - at least once, as its assets may lose safe heaven status afterwards.

Therefore, from the viewpoint of the investors from other societies, it is best to have more than one reserve currency and more than one safe heaven for their investments. And therefore, *competition is needed even for reserve currencies and safe heaven assets in the global markets, to protect the interest of global investors.* In other words, as discussed in Book Two of this series, having monopolies or over-concentration of power is not good in global financial markets either – as the dominant society may use its power to tax the rest directly or indirectly.

Indirect Taxes And Central Banks (2) : Asset Price Inflation

When individuals earn some income, they either spend it for current consumption, in which case they buy consumption goods, or save it for future consumption, in which case they buy investment assets (equities, bonds, real estate, etc). Therefore, from the viewpoint of assessing their overall purchasing power through their lifetime, the changes in the prices of both the consumption goods and the investment assets must be a matter of concern for all individuals, and thus for the society.

In practise, individuals concentrate on the changes in the prices of the consumption goods, probably because they experience the effects of these changes immediately and clearly, and thus they are familiar with the concept of *consumer price inflation (CPI).* And although they care about the overall changes in the prices of investment assets as well, due to the complex nature of the changes in the prices of these assets, they fail to notice a major component of price change that results from the printing of money[35] by the Central Banks, and thus fail to understand the concept of *asset price inflation*[36] *(API)*.

THE TROUBLE WITH THE DYNAMICS AND THE RECOGNITION OF API

Investment assets' prices change for a variety of reasons, primarily due the basic demand-supply relation based on economic conditions, which in turn is a complex function of both the current developments and the expectations for those in the future. A complete discussion of these factors is beyond the scope of this book, however, it is easy to recognise that, within that overall picture the demand side is significantly effected by the amount of money printed by the Central Banks.

In consumer goods, prices usually rise at one pace or another, and thus there usually is some inflation, making it easy to visualise the indirect-tax effect of CPI in the long run. In investment assets however, prices fluctuate in both directions more frequently and with wide margins for long periods for many reasons. Consequently, observing the effects of Central Banks' money printing on the changes in asset prices is difficult. Still, these effects can be discussed conceptually.

When a Central Bank prints money one way or another, and does that excessively (beyond that justified by the economic growth), this will create some upward pressure in the asset prices, as now there is more money in circulation chasing those assets. To reemphasize, there are many factors effecting the changes in investment asset prices, and therefore, the effect of a Central Bank's printing excessive money will merge with and may sometimes be dominated by one of these factors. Consequently, such printing of money may or may not eventually rise the overall asset prices, but the effect is still there. Therefore, it has to be kept in mind that *there will always be an asset price inflation component hidden in the overall price change, due to the Central Bank's printing excessive money.*

TAXATION AND DISTRIBUTION RESULTING FROM THE CENTRAL BANKS' PRINTING MONEY

To be able to further analyse the effects of a Central Bank's printing excessive money in the rest of this sub-section, assume that all the other potential factors effecting investment asset prices are stable or negligible.

When a Central Bank prints excessive money, it not easy to forecast whether the newly created money in the economy will primarily go to consumption or to savings. Under regular economic conditions, it will probably go primarily to consumption, and will consequently rise consumer price inflation.

However, under conditions of economic crises, like those at the aftermath of 2008, where the trust in the future of the economy hit the rock bottom and thus the desire for consumption is weakened by the fear factor, most of the printed money may flow to investment assets, and consequently create a significant asset price inflation (API) – way above the consumer price inflation (CPI).

At a period during which API is higher than CPI, those individuals who already own or can buy investment assets at the beginning of the period, will experience a rise in their purchasing power (i.e. in their consumption capability) by the end of the period, as the Central Bank *practically distributes additional wealth* to them by causing a rise in the real value of the investment assets they own[37]. However, those who do not own the investment assets when the Central Bank printed money, but will be buying them later on in the future, with their future savings to be spared out from their future earnings -which in practise rise more or less in line with the CPI-, will then have to sacrifice more of their short-term consumption capability to buy these investment assets at their much higher real prices, or alternatively, if they do not want to or can not sacrifice short-term consumption capability, they will have to buy less of these investment assets and thus will have to sacrifice their future consumption capability. Either way, they will be losing some consumption capability in real terms at one time or another, and thus are *practically being taxed* by the Central Bank's printing excessive money. Therefore, the Central Bank's printing excessive money actually results in a well-hidden taxation and distribution scheme.

To make the case more dramatic, remember that, in the usual course of an individual's lifetime, one barely earns good enough to sustain his life in his younger years, and only at his mature years starts to earn high enough to spare some savings and accumulate investment assets for his future consumption. Under this observation, when the Central Bank prints excessive money at time of a crisis, and consumer price inflation (CPI) remains relatively low while asset price inflation (API) skyrockets, the Central Bank practically rewards those who already have accumulated some investment assets, namely many of those who are in their mature years, at the expense of the young whose future consumption will now be heavily taxed through a high asset price inflation. However, any previous economic misbehaviour that had created the current crisis was not the fault of the young, but those of the mature and elderly. Therefore, this is practically taxing the young generation for the sins of the current mature or elderly generation, just exercised in disguise – and thus is terribly unfair.

A WEAK PROMISE: REVERSING THE PROCESS

As the practical taxation and distribution process resulting from the excessive money printing of a Central Bank is clearly an unfair one, whenever a Central Bank starts such a process, usually in response to an economic crisis, it almost always promises to reverse the process as the economic conditions get better at an undefined time in the future. Indeed, at least in theory, if the Central Bank decreases the money supply through various methods, which corresponds to annihilating the money printed before, investment asset prices will slow down or even may fall back, such that cumulative API will come close to cumulative CPI for the overall period. Thus, the asset holders during the initial process will lose their real benefits, while those without assets during the initial process will now have a chance to acquire investment assets at de-inflated prices, without sacrificing some of their future consumption. In short, as the initial process is reversed, the initial unfairness will be neutralised. In practise, however, there are two main problems with this promised reversal process.

First, those who will practically be taxed by the reversal process may not be the same people who have benefitted from the distribution by the initial process. Similarly, those who will benefit from the reversal process may not be those who were taxed by the initial process. To visualise why and how, consider two generations, X and Y, where X is the older and Y is the younger one. And assume that a crisis is faced in a certain year, after which excessive amounts of money is printed, and following the improvement in the economic conditions, the money printing process is reversed 20 years later. In this case, most probably generation X had savings before the initial money printing process started and thus benefitted from the distribution, while they have liquidated those savings to enjoy their elderly years, thus ended up without much investment assets when the process is reversed. Consequently, they have not been effected by any fall in the real value of investment assets during the reversal process, and escaped taxation, making them net winners. Generation Y had no savings before the initial process, thus has not benefitted from any distribution by then, and they reached their savings accumulation years after the beginning of the process and saved for say 10 years under high asset prices, at the end of which they are heavily taxed in practise by the falling prices due to the reversal of the process, making them net losers, as they got burned twice. This simple illustration reveals that reversing such a process can not be considered a fair one, but just on the contrary, may even pour fuel to the fire and increase unfairness further.

A second problem is that, on most occasions, the process will never be reversed. There are always new excuses to argue that the economy is not in a condition to tolerate the reversal of such a process and thus the Central Bank will have to wait longer. Consequently, the process may at best be reversed only partially, and its initial hidden taxation and distribution effect will survive up to a significant extent.

A FURTHER NEGATIVE EFFECT OF API IGNITED BY THE CENTRAL BANK

The discussion above has revealed one major negative effect of API caused by the excessive money printing of a Central Bank: the resulting high asset price inflation is a hidden and unfair taxation-and-distribution scheme, that corresponds to a net wealth transfer from some to the others.

A second negative effect is that, just like consumer price inflation feeding on itself due to being driven by expectations[38], the asset price inflation on investment goods also feeds on itself through expectations: the higher the recent API, the more investors expect to continue to earn on their investments in the future and consequently increase their savings and investments, therefore further rising asset prices, thus further strengthening expectations, and thus starting a cycle which enables API to feed on itself. And thus asset prices may continue to rise even though the money printing process may be slowed down, eventually creating a bubble. Unfortunately, bubbles have this habit of bursting out sooner or later, harming the economy and many times causing just another financial crisis. And in the rare cases where a bubble may fail to get burst by itself, the Central Bank may come to the rescue, and, by either terminating or reversing the money printing process, bursts the bubble.

THE TROUBLE WITH THE MISSION DEFINITION OF A CENTRAL BANK REGARDING API

As the excessive money printing of a Central Bank creates negative consequences stemming from high asset price inflation, the mission statements of Central Banks might have covered keeping API within moderate levels as well. However, as mentioned at the beginning of this sub-section, apart from a Central Bank's money printing process, investment asset prices may change for many reasons, like higher economic growth or lower risks in the economy in general, or some other changes in the demand / supply for investment assets, all of which are natural and fine. Therefore, unlike the case with CPI, a Central Bank can not be given a mission to keep API within a certain boundary. However, a Central Bank can adopt a self-made policy of voluntarily limiting its freedom to printing money within the boundaries justified by the growth in the economy in general, and in very rare occasions printing extra money only for short periods of time and at not-so-excessive amounts, in order to minimise the harm it may inflict on the economy in general.

Taxes On Future Generations : Long-Term Borrowing

Financing the budget through long-term borrowing by the state (from any lenders apart from its own Central Bank), is politically a very convenient solution, as no voter in the coming election will be paying any taxes to pay back that debt. However, as somebody has to pay back that debt someday in the future, while borrowing and spending today decreases the tax burden on the current generation, it practically shifts the tax burden to the future generations, who, as they are not yet born, have no political power and thus no way to defend their rights. In principle, therefore, this is morally unacceptable, as it increases the welfare of the current generation at the expense of the future generations. Thus, it is equivalent to cheating of the current generation against the future generations.

Once the state starts to borrow, it passes the burden of financing to the next generation. But the next generation, being brighter than the current one, will not pay it back either. Just on the contrary, they will borrow further and pass the bigger debt to their next generation. This expansion of debt will continue until one day it becomes crystal clear that the debt is not sustainable anymore.

At that point, there will be three options, all practically equivalent to punishing (i.e. taxing) some future generation for the sins (i.e. borrowing) of the previous generations:

- First, heavy direct taxation of a future generation.
- Second, paying back the debt by printing money (if the debt is in domestic currency), equivalent to indirect taxation of a future generation, as discussed above.
- Third, defaulting on the debt, equivalent to directly taxing the lenders of the debt.

The eventual choice between these options will depend on both *the currency of the debt* and *who the lenders are*.

Under certain conditions, it may be possible to pass some part of the burden to *the future generations of other societies*. Whether this should cause any ethical relief to the borrowing generation is another matter.

DECIDING THE FUTURE GENERATION TO BE TAXED: LOCAL OR FOREIGN

The way the state borrows today will determine whether the price has to be fully paid by the local future generation, or can be shared with the future generations of other societies.

If the borrowing is made in domestic currency from locals, sharing the burden with the other societies will not be possible, so the whole price will be paid by the local future generations. In practise, it will be difficult to sell the first or the third option politically, so the primary choice will most probably come out to be the second, where the indirect tax will be widely distributed in disguise.

If the borrowing is made in a foreign currency from other societies, the second option is unavailable as it is impossible to print a foreign currency. Consequently, either the first or the third or a blend of those two options will have to be used. Taxing the locals for the whole burden is not politically desirable, thus, blending in some partial default to shift some of the burden to the other societies may seem attractive in the short run. However, such behaviour may keep the defaulting state out of the global debt markets for a long time and eventually may result in an even bigger economic cost for the locals in the long run.

If the borrowing is made in a foreign currency solely from locals, again sharing the burden with the other societies will not be possible. Moreover, as it is impossible to print a foreign currency, this time the second option seems to be unavailable. However, by utilizing a nice trick involving the conversion of foreign currency denominated debt to local currency at a fixed exchange rate determined by the state, the second option becomes available in practice. Then, among all the three options, the one with the least political cost will be chosen.

Finally, if the borrowing is made in domestic currency from other societies, the situation gets further complicated, as it is both possible to choose the second option (i.e. print money) and also share the burden with the other societies. In such cases, the final choice will depend on the relative strength of the borrower versus the lenders, where such strength can stem from one or more of superior economic or political or military power.

If the borrower is relatively weaker -or at least not far stronger- than the lenders, and will continue to need their goodwill to stay in the global markets, it will prefer the first choice, provided that it can afford it. The second and third choices seem to be available in theory, but as they will result in sharing the burden with the other societies, and thus will correspond to cheating against foreign lenders, they will not be preferred unless the local economy is so weak that the first choice is inadequate beyond the control of the borrowing state. Interestingly enough, although rational thinking implies that a state with a weak economy should probably be unable to borrow in its own currency from foreigners to start with, and thus such cases should be rare, in practise they are not. The detailed analysis of how such unexpected cases emerge frequently in practice was made in Book Two of this series.

In the most common case, if the state borrowing in its own domestic currency is economically and politically stronger than the foreign lenders, and happens to be an issuer of a reserve currency, it will not prefer to use the first option (or just use it partially to save face), and it does not need the third option in practise. Its simplest choice can be the second option, namely printing money, which will conveniently provide the luxury of indirectly taxing the foreign lenders, namely the future generations of other societies. The trouble is that, if it heavily relies on this choice, the other societies will wake up to reality sooner or later, and its currency will probably lose its reliability as a reserve currency in the medium to long run, and thus this choice can practically be used just once. Therefore, rather than heavily relying on this choice, it may prefer to utilize its superior power to roll over of its debt in spite of the major accumulated risk it entails, and in the meantime utilize the second option only moderately and keep the indirect taxation of other societies' future generations in disguise, conveniently enabling its currency to keep its reserve currency status.

In short, *the societies who are the issuers of global reserve currencies and borrow from foreigners in their own currencies, have the special ability to easily shift some of their own debt burden to other societies' future generations.* And in a world where any society can ethically accept taxing their own future generations through financing their budgets with excessive local long-term borrowing, those who have the luxury to tax other societies' future generations will naturally not hesitate to utilise that chance. Therefore, foreign lenders (Central Banks, Treasuries, corporations, individuals) need to think twice before investing in the debt of any reserve currency issuer, as they may be leaving an asset to their future generations which can be taxed by the issuer of that currency in many ways.

Concluding On Types Of Taxation

The discussion in this section revealed that the indirect taxes resulting from a Central Bank's printing money and the taxes on future generations resulting from long-term borrowing are unfair in nature. Moreover, as they are not rule based, they lack the political approval of the society, making their legitimacy questionable. Even worse, their effects on income distribution (i.e. on inequality), and therefore on the overall welfare of the society, are unclear – as each application is a different case, serving one purpose or another depending on the decision of the political authority. And the worst, they do not serve the prevention of concentrations of power in the economy, but on the contrary, may even serve to further increase the already existing concentrations.

In short, fair and legitimate taxation, with clear and positive effects on inequality and the welfare of the society, requires the utilisation of direct taxes as the primary source of financing for the state budget, and the minimisation of the others. And if the approaches to direct taxation are modified in the ways discussed in the next section, they will also serve to prevent the over-concentration of powers in the economy.

5.3   Taxation Of Extreme-Success

Why Extreme-Success Should Be Further Taxed

Achieving success is the natural main goal of all competitors in any competition, and is the driving force behind the economic development of the society. However, as discussed in Book Two of this series, for social justice in principle, and for the optimisation of the allocation of resources in an economy and the maximisation of the welfare of the society in practice, success has to be obtained in an environment of Fair Competition, primarily through the utilisation of merit.

In principle, extreme-success can be a result of superior-merit, with superior wisdom and superior vision as additional ingredients, and without much contribution of good luck. However, *success-based-only-on-superior-merit has practical limits in a competitive environment. And those limits are definitely lower and stay within rational boundaries when there is Fair Competition, as no one is the one-and-only person with superior-merit in any market or society.*

In other words, individuals can win on merit, however, as no one is infinitely more merited than all the others, success-based-on-merit-alone has an upper limit in practise.

Therefore, assuming that there is no excessive risk taking or cheating, in cases where the winner of the competition absolutely crashed the rest of the competitors, such extreme-success most probably stems from extreme-good-luck, although at times there may be a component of superior-merit in it as well.

As discussed in detail in Book Two, contrary to common understanding, in such cases of extreme-success based partially on merit but fundamentally on extreme-good-luck, there is some misallocation of resources and the resulting value created for the society is not optimal in the long run.

It is also possible that extreme-success comes through pure extreme-good-luck, without much of a merit, but just because of unknowingly and thus innocently taking excessive risks. In these cases, the misallocation of resources gets worse, with more damage (with respect to the case of having some component of merit) to the economy and to the welfare of the society in the long run.

However, the absolute worst case, from the viewpoint of both social justice and allocation of resources, is where cheating is involved in attaining excessive-success.

In practise, even societies without adequate Social Intellect are aware that cheating harms their welfare in the long run, and thus Cheaters who attained extreme-success have no choice but to present themselves as winners through merit accompanied by extreme-good-luck. After all, as discussed in Book Two, *cheating is actually equivalent to creating artificial-extreme-good-luck for oneself*, one way or another. Such make-up, however, does not change either the real nature or the negative consequences of their extreme-success.

And in cases where winning through merit looks too difficult to argue, Cheaters may instead try to hide behind the illusion of having taken excessive risks and then winning through extreme-good-luck, which at least looks innocent. As explained in detail in Book Two, one common way of such cheating is seemingly taking excessive risks while knowing from the very beginning that, although the potential rewards will be kept by themselves, any potential losses can and will be transferred to others, including the society. Thus, even though there is some fake risk taking on the surface, the innocence is not there while cheating is.

CONCLUDING ON EXTREME-SUCCESS AND LUCK

The ongoing discussion reveals that, although there are many alternate paths to success usually combined with each other, *the path to extreme-success is clear: natural-extreme-good-luck (sometimes coupled with merit), or self-fabricated-extreme-good-luck, namely cheating.*

Therefore, *contrary to common understanding, any sort of extreme-success is not fair as it contains some sort of extreme-good-luck, either natural or self-fabricated, and creates a misallocation of resources that harm the welfare of the society in the long run.*

Therefore, from the viewpoint of winners and losers, *any extreme-success creates undeserved winners* (and unobserved undeserved losers as a side effect), *and therefore*, both in principle and in practise, *it should be taxed much heavier than common success.*

Notice that, although it is difficult to clearly and explicitly distinguish between natural-extreme-good-luck and self-fabricated-extreme-good-luck, in either case, extreme-success has to be taxed more heavily, and thus the main conclusion above does not change. The only difference can be that, the more Fair Competition is established, and thus the less the cheating is in the economy, the less can be the extra taxes levied on extreme-success – but they should still exist.

A CLOSER LOOK TO MISGUIDANCE OF PERCEPTION

As mentioned above, many of those who won on a combination of extreme-merit and extreme-good-luck, prefer to deny the significance of extreme-good-luck in their overall extreme-success and argue that they won just because of their superior merit. And some of their arguments really look believable on the surface. However, when a closer look is taken, together with the somewhat-difficult-to-understand dynamics of statistics, the case for the dominance of luck emerges clearly.

For instance, consider the high-tech monopolies of the recent decades: all of them were founded and grew in the United States. Their founders, who are definitely extremely-merited, were all born (or migrated at childhood and grew up) in the US as well. However, unless one happens to believe that extremely-merited individuals can only be born in the US, it is easy to see that if these extremely-merited founders were born elsewhere, they would not have attained such extreme-success – as the necessary external conditions in which such high-tech monopolies could emerge do not exist elsewhere. But being born in the US (or migrating to US at childhood) is not an act of merit, but just good luck. However, the lack of such good luck practically eliminates 95% of the global population from the very beginning, independent of how extreme their individual merit might be. Still, a further question may come to mind: considering the remaining 5%, there are 325 million people in the US, but only a few succeeded to establish such global high-tech monopolies. Can it still be argued that their extreme-success is dominated by extreme-good-luck? Or is it more rational to believe that there are only a handful of extremely-merited individuals among the 325 million people in the US, and consequently their extreme-success is solely a result of their extreme-merit? To get a feeling for the answer, an illustrative example on the dynamics of statistics can be helpful.

DYNAMICS OF LUCK: A GAME OF HEADS AND TAILS

Consider a common game of Heads and Tails, played by very many competitors. In this game, all the competitors are divided into pairs, and each player in a pair makes a guess (bet) on whether the spilled coin will land on its head or tail. After each round of the game, the losers are eliminated, and the winners proceed to the next round where they will be paired with other remaining winners, to play another round. Assume that there are approximately 1 billion competitors at the beginning[39]. After the first round, half of the players will be eliminated, and approximately 500 million will be left. After the second round, half of the remaining players will be eliminated, and approximately 250 million will be left. After the third round, half of the remaining players will be eliminated, and approximately 125 million will be left. As the game proceeds this way, after the 29th round only 2 players will be left. And at the 30th and final round, one player will eventually win the game.

Now consider the case of the eventual winner: he succeeded to win a game where 1 billion people competed, and all except him have lost/failed. Or, from another viewpoint, he managed to guess the correct side of the tossed coin in 30 consecutive bets. The probability of someone making 30 consecutive correct bets in this game is one in a billion, or numerically 0.0000001%. Can that be just luck, or does he have some superior merit in guessing the correct side whenever a coin is tossed?

As mathematicians know well, this eventual winner's chances of winning in another toss is just 50% - just like anybody else, as he no special merit at all. By the nature of the design of the game, whenever this game is played, somebody will definitely make 30 correct choices consecutively and win. However, each time the game is played from the very beginning, with the same players, the eventual winner will be different. Never the same person twice. All winning 30 consecutive rounds, and all have a simple 50% chance to win in any next round. In short, the winners of any of these games have no special superior merit, but just extreme-good-luck on their side *just for once*, which was enough for them to win. Probability behaves in ways difficult to understand at first sight.

As this simple illustration reveals, *solely the fact that there are just a few winners in an open competition among a very large number of competitors, does not necessarily mean that the winners have won on merit.* By the nature of probability, *sometimes events may align in such a way that the reason behind the extreme-success is pure good luck.*

And life sometimes works like such a game. *Being at the right place at the right time makes all the difference – at least among otherwise equals.*

The illustration above is clearly a case of pure luck, as it is impossible to argue that the eventual outcome is dominated by merit. However, as mentioned many times before, in real life merit and luck are combined to result in a certain outcome, and it is practically difficult to isolate the components of merit and luck from each other. But still two main conclusions have to be kept in mind.

First, *in cases of extreme-success, there is almost always a component of extreme-good-luck (natural or self-fabricated).* To reemphasize, *this does not mean that there is no component of extreme-merit in extreme-success in practise, but just that extreme-good-luck has a dominant effect on the outcome.*

Second, as no case is crystal clear in practise, *those who have achieved extreme-success, almost always argue that their success is primarily based on their extreme-merit, rather than luck.*

A GLIMPSE OF REAL LIFE CASES

Going back to the recent cases of high-tech monopolies, it is now possible to explain the situation more rationally. The emergence of such high-tech companies, and their products and services, are definitely the result of the extreme-merit of their founders. However, their reaching global monopoly status, before all the other potential rivals, is a matter of extreme-good-luck.

Indeed, history of scientific development is full of inventions that are made simultaneously by many scientists at different places without even knowing each other. A similar story is valid for all the high-tech developments and innovations of the recent decades. If any of the current founders of global high-tech monopolies has not ever been born, somebody else would have developed that product or service sooner or later. However, they happened to be the ones who made it at the right place (in the US rather than in another smaller or less developed market) and at the right time (may be a few months before some others in the US market). Therefore, they definitely have some superior merit, but what differentiated them from the others with similar superior merit was their extreme-good-luck on being at the right place at the right time. And the nature of the US market (relative to the other markets) in terms of infrastructure and economic power, has enabled them to become global monopolies and prevent the emergence of other competition elsewhere, at least for a too long time. Indeed, if any of the founders of those extremely-successful corporations were born at a different place at a different time, in spite of their extreme-merit, their chances of becoming one of the world's most wealthy people would be nil.

EXTREME-SUCCESS FROM THE VIEWPOINT OF CONCENTRATION OF ECONOMIC POWER AND ITS CONSEQUENCES

As discussed above, as extreme-success primarily stems from extreme-good-luck, serving social justice and diminishing the negative effects of misallocation of resources are two fundamental reasons that require its further taxation. However, as clearly revealed by the high-tech case above, there is an even more important reason.

As discussed in Book Two of this series, extreme-success usually results in a *concentration of economic power* in its market. Even if extreme-success was originally attained through merit and/or luck, after reaching the concentration stage it almost always invites various ways of *cheating* to grow further at the expense of the society. These include rising barriers to entry for any potential competitors, higher pricing of sorts (monetary or data based) for customers, and lower pricing for suppliers, including labour. The trouble here is that, especially in cases where the extreme-success comes with an innovation creating a new product or service, the society mostly concentrates on enjoying the new product or service, and fails to remember that if this new product or service were supplied under conditions of Fair Competition instead of a concentrated economic power (i.e. a monopoly), it would be of an even higher quality offered at a lower price.

Going back to the recent high-tech global monopolies case for instance, if there were conditions of Fair Competition, and the same high-tech products and services were supplied within competitive markets by competitors of more or less equivalent economic strength, the overall outcome in terms of the quality of these services, the pricing of these services (in terms of personal information gathered), and their contribution to the economic growth of the economies would have been much better. However, as these products and services made significant contributions to everybody's daily life, the trouble with their being monopolies is not discussed much. The society considers that life would have been worse without those products and services, but unfortunately fails to remember how everything would have been better if those products and services were offered under competitive conditions rather than by monopolies.

Finally, again as discussed in Book Two, as extreme-success increases its economic power, it will have to get political support - at least in terms of having advantageous legislation and preventing any changes that may weaken its status, both of which are against the best interests of the society. And for that purpose it needs to influence political decision making, or even cooperate with concentrated political powers. And that requires having extreme financial power. And exactly for that reason, in all the cases where there are inadequate Fair Competition and monopolies with extreme economic powers emerge, their economic power and thus their potential political influence should be diluted through further taxation.

Needless to say, the trouble with extreme-success and its consequences is not confined to high-tech markets. Just on the contrary, *as globalisation and technological developments enable the emergence of concentrated economic powers or global monopolies in very many sectors, the trouble is fast spreading in the economies and in the political systems of all western societies.*

A WELCOME SIDE EFFECT: FINANCING OF THE STATE BUDGET

The further taxation of extreme-success for all the fundamental reasons discussed above will also rise the direct tax revenues for the state budget, and decrease the need for indirect taxation or heavy long-term borrowing resulting in the taxation of the future generations.

IN CONCLUSION

Wrapping-up the discussion in this sub-section, the main reasons for further taxation of extreme-success, *from the most important to the least in practice,* are:

- Preventing concentrations of economic power and resulting political influence against the interests of the society
- Improving allocation of resources (i.e. limiting the misallocation of resources) to maximise economic growth and welfare
- Creating extra revenue through direct taxes for the state budget
- Serving social justice

Any society with adequate Social Intellect will therefore choose to implement further taxation for extreme-success, in several forms to be discussed in the rest of this section.

Types Of Economic Inequality

In the previous chapters, economic inequality was examined considering only income inequality. However, there are actually three types of economic inequality: consumption inequality, income inequality and wealth inequality.

CONSUMPTION INEQUALITY

From the viewpoint of individuals, the one that matters most and that is easiest to observe is consumption inequality.

Thanks to the latest developments in digital communication technologies that enabled the free flow of information, everybody at every corner of a society, or of the world for that matter, now knows how others are consuming in their society or in other societies. This makes consumption inequality easily observable, and such awareness makes the removal of it politically demandable.

The sources of any consumption inequality are income or wealth inequalities, and therefore, in principle, consumption inequality will rise as the others rise, and will fall as the others fall. The practise, however, is not so. Even when income or wealth inequalities are rising, it is possible to contain consumption inequality, or even decrease it further, simply by allowing more borrowing by those who fell behind and let them consume somewhat more and consequently feel less unequal. And, as low consumption inequality is easy to observe, while changes in income or wealth inequalities are not, such borrowing driven consumption will delay any widespread political demand for the correction of the rising income or wealth inequalities.

Unfortunately, when income gaps are not narrowing (or rising), decreasing consumption gaps through borrowing is not a sustainable solution in the long run, as sooner or later excessive leverage will accumulate in the system, and one day the system will eventually collapse, as it did in 2008. Then, consumption inequality will suddenly skyrocket, and as the society faces the reality, some sort of political reaction will emerge. Depending on the level of inequalities, and thus on the severity of the economic crisis, even the stability of the social order of the society may fall in danger.

Therefore, *any society with adequate Social Intellect should care about any excessive rise in income or wealth inequalities hiding behind any borrowing-enabled-consumption, and take the necessary steps to cure them before facing an economic or political crisis.*

INCOME INEQUALITY

As discussed in Chapter 4, in principle, the best solution for containing income inequality within optimal (thus moderate and acceptable) levels is establishing Fair Competition to prevent excessive income inequality before taxation, and then utilizing only marginal taxation-and-distribution to achieve the desired after-tax inequality level.

In practice, however, establishing Fair Competition requires a high level of Social Intellect for any society, and thus can not be achieved fully at any western society at least in the foreseeable future. Therefore, cases of extreme-success, and consequently too much of a rise in income inequality will be common. Some further taxation beyond the regular levels is required for such cases.

WEALTH INEQUALITY

In practise, wealth inequality is *accumulated income inequality* over the long run.

Consequently, wealth inequality can not be contained unless income inequality is contained first. However, this necessary condition, even if satisfied, is not enough for two reasons. First, even acceptable levels of income inequality for the short run, may accumulate to create excessive-wealth-inequality in the long run. And second, as wealth earns an income by itself, even after the taxation of such income, wealth will continue to build up on itself, and therefore, in cases where wealth inequality is already too high, it can not be decreased unless some further taxation on extreme-wealth is applied.

EXTREME-SUCCESS RESULTING IN EXCESSIVE INEQUALITIES

Extreme-success, and the concentrated economic power it creates, may result in an extreme-income stream for a long period, and consequently an extreme accumulation of wealth resulting from such prolonged extreme-income. Therefore, extreme-success creates both excessive-income-inequality and excessive-wealth-inequality, both harmful for the welfare of the society in the long run, as discussed before.

Structural changes on the taxation of both extreme-income and extreme-wealth are therefore necessary to be able to cope with these negative effects of extreme-success.

Extreme-Income Taxes

In the western societies on both coasts of the Atlantic, the current brackets for income taxes are mostly similar to each other[40], with the topmost bracket for approximately $ 250.000 and above, taxed around 40%.

This topmost bracket implicitly makes two assumptions. First, that there are not very many people who earn more than $250.000, which is usually true when measured in proportion to the total population. Second, and more important, that those who are above the top bracket still earn in the vicinity of $250.000, say up to $400.000, which can not be further away from reality.

As discussed above, globalisation and technological developments enable the emergence of concentrated economic powers in very many sectors, at unprecedented scales, where the winners earn incomes way beyond the rationale of the second assumption above. Consequently, the tax brackets and tax rates for income taxes have to be modified to serve the most critical needs mentioned above – namely preventing concentrations of economic power and their potential political influence, and improving allocation of resources to maximise growth. This can be achieved simply by adding further brackets and higher rates, as illustrated below.

INCOME BRACKETS (on Annual Income)	TAX RATES
0 – up to $ 50.000	10%
$ 50.000 to $ 100.000	25%
$ 100.000 to $ 250.000	35%
$ 250.000 to $ 1 million	45%
$ 1 million to $ 3 million	55%
Above $ 3 million	65%

The brackets and rates in the table above are just introduced to illustrate the logic of taxing extreme-success further. Needless to say, each society should adjust their own brackets and rates with respect to their own economic conditions[41] and social norms[42].

The common argument used to oppose the introduction of such higher brackets with higher tax rates, is that, too-high tax rates will decrease the motivation of the taxed and consequently will decrease the economic growth rate in the long run. Indeed, if too high tax rates were applied for common success, the argument would have been correct. However, first, the new brackets introduced above effect only a very small proportion of the society (probably below 1%), and thus there is no general demotivating effect – but just on the contrary, there will be a positive motivation effect arising from the fall of too high after-tax inequality. Second, and more important, those who are effected by the new high brackets probably have other reasons to be motivated – rather than further after-tax income. Remembering the marginal utility / diminishing returns phenomenon presented in Sections 1.3 and 4.4, it is easy to see that anybody earning above $ 3 million a year (in the illustration) is probably getting his satisfaction from other dimensions of success, like recognition, status, power or whatever other ambitions, and thus will not lose much of a motivation for being taxed further. In other words, if somebody is earning above $ 3 million for many years in a row, he will either quit work and enjoy himself for the rest of his life (independent of the tax rates), or, in line with his other ambitions, will continue to work, probably as hard as he can. Thus, the loss of motivation argument regarding the further taxation of extreme-success is hard to sell rationally, and even harder to sell politically.

Finally, if societies fail to tax extreme-income (and to decrease too-high income inequality), they naturally fuel the emergence of extreme-wealth, and consequently excessive-wealth-inequality. And then, the society will have to choose between living in an excessively unequal economic environment which will sooner or later cause social unease and endanger the sustainability of the social order, or trying to cure excessive economic inequality through heavy taxation of extreme-wealth, which is more controversial and more difficult to implement in practise on such a wide scale. But if extreme-income is rationally taxed to start with, the emergence of extreme-wealth will be contained, and even if the need for the taxation of extreme-wealth still arises, its implementation will be relatively easier as much fewer people will need to be effected.

CONSUMPTION TAXES

The discussion above has focused on the need for Extreme-Income Taxes, from the viewpoints of concentrations of economic power and their potential political influence, and improving allocation of resources to maximise growth. However, the third reason for the application of further taxes on extreme-success, namely creating extra revenue through direct taxes for the state budget, is also important.

When the society fails to implement the appropriate Extreme-Income Tax scheme, it has no choice left but to resort to other kinds of direct taxes to finance the budget of the state. The most common one is the *consumption tax*, also called value added tax to make it more incomprehensible, which is somewhat unfair for two reasons. First, it is applied on the consumption of the individuals financed by their already-taxed-income. Second, and worse, *it is not progressive*, meaning that everybody pays the same amount of tax for the same unit of consumption, independent of their income. Consequently, *it increases the wealth inequality within the society:* as the poor spend a higher ratio of their after-income-tax-revenue, the burden of the non-progressive consumption tax on spending will take away a higher proportion of their revenues, which means that they will have less savings left that will accumulate to become their future wealth[43].

Therefore, consumption tax is practically equivalent to a wealth tax applied more heavily to the poor, making it very unfair. Unfortunately, the collection of consumption taxes is easy, and the amounts collected are comparable to income taxes in many cases, so the states love them. The fair solution, however, would be taxing extreme-wealth resulting from extreme-success.

Extreme-Wealth Taxes

Wealth is accumulated savings, which are the part of income left after consumption. When income reaches extreme levels, the proportion of consumption within income falls to negligible levels, and practically most of the income is saved. Extreme-wealth, therefore, is the accumulation of extreme-income.

It is clear that the continuation of extreme-income will further increase extreme-wealth. However, contrary to initial intuition, the loss of extreme-income does not decrease extreme-wealth. Once extreme-wealth passes beyond a certain boundary, it will earn an investment income of its own and feed on itself, and consequently it will not decrease even if the extreme-income which initially fuelled it disappears. In other words, if and when extreme-income is curbed by the establishment of Fair Competition or through Extreme-Income Taxes mentioned above, on the one hand, the emergence of new extreme-wealth may be prevented or at least slowed down, but on the other hand, the previously accumulated extreme-wealth will be unaffected. Therefore, the introduction of Extreme-Wealth Taxes is necessary to curb the already accumulated extreme-wealth.

FROM THE VIEWPOINT OF INEQUALITY

To further clarify the trouble, the analyses above can also be made through the viewpoint of inequality. Excessive wealth inequality initially stems from persistent excessive income inequality. However, excessive wealth inequality can not be cured through eliminating excessive income inequality. Just on the contrary, excessive wealth inequality will actually be stabilised (or even worsened) through eliminating excessive income inequality. This is simply because, as the elimination of excessive income inequality prevents the accumulation of *new* extreme-wealth, it will lock in the current status of the existing extreme-wealth owners. And the existing extreme-wealth owners will continue to earn income on their already accumulated wealth, which will increase the overall wealth inequality even further to their benefit in the long run.

In short, *introducing Extreme-Income Taxes without introducing Extreme-Wealth Taxes, will only benefit the current holders of extreme-wealth, and therefore, will not result in the desired decrease in the excessive wealth inequality within the society*. For that reason, *any society with adequate Social Intellect will introduce Extreme-Income Taxes and Extreme-Wealth Taxes together*.

THE TROUBLE WITH EXTREME-WEALTH

As extreme-wealth feeds on itself, it is more persistent in the long run with respect to extreme-income. As explained above, under conditions of Fair Competition and/or high levels of taxation-and-distribution, although extreme-income is somewhat tamed, the existing extreme-wealth remains intact or even grows. For that reason, *in almost all societies, the concentration of wealth within the society tends to be higher than the concentration of income*.

The final nail on the coffin is that, *as extreme-wealth is more concentrated and therefore stronger, its political influence to protect and promote itself is also much stronger*. That, in turn, makes the negative effects of excessive wealth inequality on the welfare of the society much worse than those of excessive income inequality. And by the same token, it becomes necessary to care to decrease excessive wealth inequality together with excessive income inequality.

THE TROUBLE WITH THE INVESTMENT INCOME OF EXTREME-WEALTH

All savings are invested in one way or another, however the rates of return on them are not identical. A well known dimension that creates a difference in returns is the risk taking appetite of the investor. However, another dimension, less known but still critical, is the overall size of the investment. When investments are of a much larger size, the financial services and the types of products offered are practically different. And higher amounts and a higher risk taking capacity usually enable participation in private markets and deals, and reach attractive opportunities that may be inaccessible to common investors, without facing much of a competition and consequently earning high returns. To cut the long story short, the returns on investments are higher for extreme-wealth with respect to common cases, at equivalent risk appetites.

This practically means that, *in the long run extreme-wealth grows faster than average wealth, and therefore curbing excessive wealth inequality requires much higher tax rates on extreme-wealth than generally discussed in public.*

This requirement makes establishing extreme-wealth-taxes a radical change in the social contract of the society, and needless to say, will require a higher level of Social Intellect than most societies currently have.

HOW EXTREME-WEALTH TAXES HAVE TO BE STRUCTURED

Defining a tax scheme requires defining its tax brackets and the tax rates for those brackets. These definitions, however, have to be time and condition dependent, and therefore has to be decided and managed by each society separately. The general structure presented below is just given to clarify the underlying rationale behind such taxes.

THE TAX BRACKETS

To define the tax brackets for the taxation of extreme-wealth, a *threshold for extreme-wealth* has to be defined first. As wealth is accumulated income, it will be rational to tie this threshold for extreme-wealth to the income per capita of a society.

While doing so, it is important to keep in mind that, the primary aim of establishing Extreme-Wealth Taxes is to prevent concentrations of economic power and their potential political influence. Keeping this aim at the focus of the structure is necessary in determining the extreme-wealth threshold, the tax brackets and the corresponding tax rates.

In common private applications of our day, the definition of an ultra-high-net-worth-individual in the jargon starts from $ 50 million. That level, however, is unnecessarily low for the primary aim of these taxes.

To decide an appropriate threshold level for extreme-wealth based on the income per capita of a society, a limit for extreme-success has to be defined. For the illustrative structure that will be given below, an individual earning 50 times the average (after-tax) income will be considered extremely successful[44]. And in line with the common life-spans and work-spans of our day, this extremely successful individual is assumed to work for 40 years during which he consistently earned such an income and saved it all. Combining these assumptions, the threshold for extreme-wealth can be defined as shown below.

Threshold for extreme-wealth =

> = (Income per Capita)*(50 times success)*(40 years of work-life)

> = (Income per Capita)*2.000

To visualize, for a society with an income per capita of $50.000, the threshold for extreme-wealth comes out to be $ 100 million. For a society with an income per capita of $75.000, the threshold for extreme-wealth comes out to be $ 150 million, etc.

Once the threshold for extreme-wealth is set this way, the progressive brackets for Extreme-Wealth Taxes can be constructed accordingly. Continuing the illustration above, these brackets can be as shown in the table below.

As these brackets are based on income per capita, whenever income per capita rises due to economic growth, or inflation, or for any reason, the brackets will also rise to reflect it.

The way progressive taxation works is well known from the application of common income taxes. Still, it is important to remind that, any individual whose wealth is below the extreme-wealth threshold will not pay any tax on his wealth, and anyone with some wealth above the threshold, will only be taxed on the portion of his wealth above the threshold. Therefore, *the Extreme-Wealth Tax can not ever decrease anybody's wealth below the threshold level*.

TAX BRACKETS (m: million)		
Tax Bracket in Principle	For a society with income/capita : $50.000	For a society with income/capita : $75.000
Up to Threshold	Up to $ 100m	Up to $ 150m
(Threshold) to (2xThreshold)	$100m - $200m	$150m - $300m
(2xThreshold) to (5xThreshold)	$200m - $500m	$300m - $750m
Above (5xThreshold)	Above $500m	Above $750m

TAX RATES

As mentioned above, extreme-wealth grows faster than average wealth, and therefore curbing excessive wealth inequality requires tax rates high enough to have any practical effect.

When extreme-wealth is taxed, it decreases annually at an amount of "tax on extreme-wealth minus earnings on extreme-wealth". In other words, unless the Extreme-Wealth Tax rate is higher than the investment return on extreme-wealth, the accumulated amount of wealth will never decrease, but just continue to increase at a slower speed.

If the sole target of the Extreme-Wealth Tax were to create financing for the budget, any tax rate above zero would have served some purpose[45]. However, if the target is to decrease excessive wealth inequality, then a tax rate much higher than the rate of return on the investment is needed. And if the target is the prevention of political influence, then the tax rate to be applied above some multiple of the threshold must be high enough to decrease such extreme-wealth within a rational period of time. And a rational period of time can not be decades.

For illustration, consider the simple annual tax rates in the table below for the brackets mentioned above. It is possible to have a dynamic setting for these annual tax rates[46] -based on variables like potential returns on investment, inflation, and the structure of income taxes-, but this simple scheme is enough for illustrative purposes.

TAX BRACKET	ANNUAL EXTREME-WEALTH TAX RATE
Up to Threshold	No Tax
(Threshold) to (2xThreshold)	10%
(2xThreshold) to (5xThreshold)	15%
Above (5xThreshold)	20%

Needless to say, the final bracket, which is the critical one from the viewpoint of preventing the over-concentration of economic power and its potential political influence, corresponds to an actual upper limit on the maximum wealth that is allowed in practise in the society, in the long run. In other words, if the final bracket is used with the corresponding high tax rate, assuming the return on investments will remain below that rate in the long run, all extreme-wealth will decrease towards the "5 times threshold" limit eventually.

As there are no significant wealth taxes in any society yet, and thus there is no upper limit to how much wealth can be accumulated, such a new approach to set an upper boundary on the maximum wealth that can be attained, corresponds to a radical change in the social contract of the society, and thus requires a high level of Social Intellect to be politically demanded. In short, the last bracket, or even the last two brackets, may remain to be just a thought exercise for the foreseeable future, as any society with a current level of inadequate Social Intellect is not expected to establish such a taxation structure.

Focusing on the tax rates, at first sight, these nice round numbers that came out of thin air for illustration, may seem to be aggressive. However, as the extreme-wealth will earn an income, the net effect of these tax rates will be severely diluted. In fact, the first bracket above the threshold may not even decrease the real value (and thus the economic power and the potential political influence) of the extreme-wealth at all. In fact, if the return on the investments is high, the extreme-wealth will continue to rise in real terms in spite of the tax.

Indeed, if the return on the investments is high enough, which is not an uncommon case, especially in the winner-takes-it-all markets of our day, it may take a very long time even for the higher rates at the higher brackets to have any meaningful effect[47].

POTENTIAL VIOLATION OF THE UPPER BOUNDARY IN SPITE OF HIGH TAX RATES

In cases where extreme-wealth emerges from the fast accumulation of extreme-income based on the introduction of some new innovative products or services that result in a heavy creative destruction in the markets, just like the high-tech cases of the recent past, extreme-wealth will grow faster than it can be taxed away even with the aggressive rates given above, even in the medium run. Consequently, the upper boundary mentioned above may be broken upwards and stay violated for a very long time.

In principle, the returns on all investments will eventually fall back towards rational levels and thus the highest tax rates will sooner or later make all extreme-wealth shrink back towards the upper boundary. In practise, however, the extreme-wealth is bright enough to notice this fact and act accordingly: concentrated economic powers almost always go for political influence to protect themselves.

OBSTACLES TO IMPLEMENTATION

As can be guessed from the ongoing discussion, there are many obstacles to the implementation of Extreme-Wealth Taxes in the structure described above. Among the most outstanding obstacles are:

- lack of political demand by society for the necessary taxes
- political influence of extreme-wealth against being taxed
- international competition for lowering current taxes, rather than coordination for implementing the missing ones
- practical difficulties in measuring wealth, worsened by the deliberate efforts of the financial sector to hide extreme-wealth through innovative structures

LACK OF POLITICAL DEMAND BY THE SOCIETY

The inescapable integration of economies (aided by the advancements in technology) created global markets, which in turn created concentrated economic powers on a global scale. Consequently, extreme-wealth can now reach never before seen levels, with never before seen political influence or even power. Consequently, the need for curbing extreme-wealth is more important now than it has ever been. And any society with adequate Social Intellect should have already demanded the dilution and limitation of such economic and eventually political concentrations of power.

Unfortunately, as mentioned above, the introduction of Extreme-Wealth Taxes with the structure described above corresponds to a radical change in the social contract of the society, and therefore requires a heavy political demand by the society that can only follow a high level of social awareness. And such social awareness can only develop when the reasons for such a change, discussed by the beginning of this section, are well communicated to the society. Only when the society realises that such a change is inevitable for the prevention of concentrations of economic power that heavily harm the interests of the society, it can have a serious political demand for the taxation of extreme-wealth.

POLITICAL INFLUENCE OF EXTREME-WEALTH

Although the society may not be intellectual enough to demand such changes yet, extreme-wealth is definitely well aware of its own interests and determined to defend them with all its power and influence.

One dimension is the direct influence of extreme-wealth on politicians and bureaucrats of the state. As discussed in Book Two of this series, this may range from misguiding them, to cooperating with them for mutual interests, or even all the way to corrupting them. But all these efforts will face practical difficulties in case the society is intellectual enough to protect its own interests.

Consequently, the second dimension has to be, and is, misguiding the society to misevaluate its own interests. In doing so, the simple common approach is to mispresent any required *Extreme-Wealth Taxes*, simply as *wealth taxes*, such that anybody with some savings will feel that he may be subject to these taxes and lose some of his hard earned wealth. The crucial difference, that any Extreme-Wealth Tax will be applied to only the amount of wealth above a certain very high threshold, say $ 150.000.000 as in the illustration above, is conveniently forgotten to be mentioned. And if the society swallows the bait, as a society with inadequate Social Intellect always does, it will reject any such proposal without any further discussion. Needless to say, the extreme-wealth threshold is so high that, in fact, much less than 0.1% of the population will be subject to any Extreme-Wealth Taxes in practise. And the targeted upper boundary on extreme-wealth, say $ 750.000.000 as in the illustration above, is so sky-high that only a few number of people will be effected.

The first step in developing an awareness in the society, rather than a fear of the misunderstood, is to appropriately call such taxes as Extreme-Wealth Taxes. Then may follow a rational discussion, resulting in some political demand.

A Matter Of Real Concern

In the discussion above, Extreme-Wealth Taxes have been examined only from the viewpoint of the society, who happens to be the tax collecting side. On the tax paying side, there are the extremely wealthy individuals, with concerns of their own, one of which is fair and rational.

The backbone of the fairness of Extreme-Wealth Taxes is that, these taxes will be applied only to the wealth above an extreme-wealth threshold. However, the definition of that threshold is vague in principle, and can only be defined in practise, as done in the illustrative case. The valid and rational concern of the extremely wealthy is that, once an Extreme-Wealth Tax starts to be applied, there is a risk that these thresholds can be set unfairly low sometime later. To make matters worse, tax rates may also be pushed too high. For instance, some populist politicians may push the limits too far and the society may lack adequate Social Intellect to reject an over-dose of such wealth taxes. This will not only make Extreme-Wealth Taxes unfair and unacceptable, but will also bring more harm than benefit to all the society as discussed in Chapter 1, and may even endanger the stability of the social order as discussed in Chapter 2.

Therefore, on the one hand, the extremely wealthy are right to fear that if such exaggerated Extreme-Wealth Taxes are applied, an economic and political system breakdown may follow. However, on the other hand, having no Extreme-Wealth Taxes (or additional Extreme-Income Taxes), and eventually driving economic inequality through the roof, will also result in such a system breakdown sooner or later. The answer, as usual, is in finding the right balance regarding the taxation of extreme-success in general, which can only be possible by rising the Social Intellect of the society to adequate levels. It is, therefore, at the best interest of everybody, including the extremely wealthy, to rise the intellectual level of the society, rather than trying to keep the society as naïve as possible.

INTERNATIONAL COMPETITION RATHER THAN COORDINATION

Regarding both Extreme-Wealth Taxes and Extreme-Income Taxes, there is very limited cooperation between societies[48], but just on the contrary, many societies compete with others through lowering all sorts of tax rates, or even eliminating taxes, to attract the extremely wealthy to their societies and their wealth to their economies.

At first sight, attracting wealth seems to bring economic advantages in the short run, such as higher local consumption and investments, and at least higher consumption taxes. By the same token, losing wealth may mean loss of such economic benefits, in addition to the loss of regular income taxes.

However, as discussed before, extreme-wealth seeks potential political influence (to the benefit of its own and against the interests of the society) sooner or later, and therefore, the departure of such wealth will also mean the disappearance of such political influence or at least the weakening of it. This hidden but major benefit will outweigh the explicit economic disadvantages of departing wealth in the long run. Similarly, if the relocating extreme-wealth stabilizes in some other society, it will seek political influence there sooner or later, harming the interests of that society in the long run, and thus outweighing its initial explicit economic advantages. Unfortunately, the societies that try to attract extreme-wealth are either unaware of this hidden trouble due to their inadequate Social Intellect, or are simply not functioning democracies where the interest of the society may have any importance.

The best solution to preventing the potential political influence of extreme-wealth anywhere, is the establishment of the Extreme-Wealth Taxes in every society through global cooperation. That, however, seems to be impossible in the foreseeable future.

The question, therefore, is, under the current conditions of global competition for attracting extreme-wealth, should the economically advanced western societies worry about losing extreme-wealth to other societies and thus delay the implementation of any extreme-wealth (or extreme-income) taxes, or should they proceed with the taxation of extreme-success and let some wealth leave. And the answer, in practise, depends on balancing the two evils: the negative consequences of the potential political influence of extreme-wealth on the interests of the society in the long run (if not taxed), versus, the explicit negative consequences of departing wealth in the short run (if taxed).

The crucial observation here is that, the explicit negative consequences of departing wealth in the short run depends on the amount of wealth that may potentially leave. If not much of a wealth will leave in spite of the establishment of Extreme-Wealth Taxes, then, on the one hand the short-term negative consequences will be limited, and on the other hand, the long-term purpose will be served, and thus the choice becomes clear: proceed to implement Extreme-Wealth Taxes.

Therefore, the critical question is how much wealth will leave in case Extreme-Wealth Taxes are established. To answer this question, it is important to remember that when wealth departs for another society, it leaves its current jurisdiction in the western world, and arrives at another jurisdiction, where, in practise, the rule of law may not be that reliable. And as extreme-wealth is well aware, although it does not like to confess explicitly, moving to a society where the rule of law is not dominant is not a rational choice – as all the wealth can be lost while trying to escape partial taxation. In other words, extreme-wealth knows very well that, it is important to pay less taxes, but it is much more important to be in a society where the rule of law reigns. Taking political risks to escape economic costs is not a rational move, and extreme-wealth is too bright to fail to see that.

What this means in practise is that, *if the western societies on both coasts of the Atlantic can cooperate among themselves regarding the taxation of extreme-wealth, even if some other societies try to attract wealth by not cooperating, the flow of wealth outside the western world will be limited. Consequently, there will be no need to balance any evils, and extreme-wealth (and extreme-income) taxes can be established.*

Otherwise, each society will have to decide on its own regarding the implementation of Extreme-Wealth Taxes, and sooner or later face the negative consequences, one way or another.

PRACTICAL DIFFICULTIES IN THE MEASUREMENT OF WEALTH

An all-inclusive definition of wealth, covering all the assets an individual may have, will make the measurement of the value of that wealth practically impossible. Fortunately, when examined from the viewpoint of economic power, potential political influence and allocation of economic resources, the definition can be simplified and limited to cover only real estate and financial assets, net of debts. Any other hard or soft assets (like pieces of art, etc.) can be neglected for practical purposes, as it is difficult to utilise them to have political influence.

Within this definition, the relatively trickier part is the financial assets. Although common assets like equities, bonds, precious metals, all sorts of investment funds, etc., are easier to handle, some complicated structured products that are deliberately designed by the financial system to hide wealth and escape taxation may require closer attention.

One other difficulty in the taxation of wealth is that, by definition, it has to include the taxation of the so-called unrealised capital gains on financial assets. These generally refer to the accumulated increases of value on the assets that are not cashed-in yet, and thus not recognised as profits from the viewpoint of income taxes. And exactly for that reason, a major portion of extreme-wealth is kept in the form of unrealised capital gains within the financial system, even in the long run, and even for generation after generation, through the utilisation of many innovative financial structures.

Needless to say, it is not possible to deal with concentrations of economic power and their potential political influence, or to optimise economic inequality in general, unless Extreme-Wealth Taxes are introduced such that unrealised capital gains are also taxed. However, by definition, unrealised capital gains are not locked in, in the sense that they not only rise in time but may also fall. And in cases where such unrealised capital gains happen to be high at the time of taxation, but fall afterwards, the effective rate of taxation may come out to be much higher than intended. To deal with this trouble, the amount of wealth that will be taken as the base for taxation can calculated as a moving average, say by taking the average value for the last five years.

In short, although practical difficulties may arise for the first time such taxes are applied, practical solutions will follow soon, as long as there is the political determination to implement and sustain Extreme-Wealth Taxes. On the one hand, better regulation can limit the financial structures devised for tax evasion purposes, and on the other hand, advanced accounting techniques can deal with their valuation better. Once there is a will to tax extreme-wealth, there will be adequate ways to handle the valuation part.

Extreme-Inheritance Taxes

Inheritance is the second most unfair way of increasing one's income and/or wealth (after cheating), as it is a matter of pure luck in terms of being born to the right family. However, looking from the viewpoint of the deceased, it is a natural right to transfer their lifetime savings to their next generation. Therefore, taxation of inheritance has to be structured to satisfy both viewpoints.

Lower amounts of inheritance, by definition, correspond to just a mediocre amount of luck, which is a natural part of life. Therefore, the right of the deceased to transfer their savings may dominate the structure at low amounts, practically meaning that the taxation of inheritance should be minimal.

Extreme-inheritance, however, is a different story. It corresponds to a case of extreme-good-luck, resulting in extreme-success with no component of merit in it. As the discussion by the beginning of this section revealed, such extreme-success based on pure good luck has to be taxed heavily.

THE STRUCTURE

Inheritance, on the one hand, is a transfer of wealth from one generation to the next. On the other hand, it is a one-time income for the receivers. The taxation of inheritance, therefore, can be structured by combining the rationale for income and wealth taxes.

To create an illustrative structure, to the benefit of the inheritance receivers, assume that inheritance is received at one's early 40's, and one lives beyond his 90's. Therefore, the transferred wealth corresponds to 50 years of income accumulated into a single payment. And then the income-tax brackets and rates used in the illustration in the relevant subsection above can be modified (i.e. tax brackets are just multiplied by 50) and used, as shown below. However, remembering the right of the deceased to pass their wealth to the next generations, societies may prefer to nullify the tax rate on the first two brackets, and start taxation at and above the third bracket.

Needless to say, each society should adjust their own brackets and rates with respect to their own economic conditions and social norms.

INHERITANCE BRACKETS	INHERITANCE TAX RATES
0 – up to $ 5 million	0%
$ 2.5 million to $ 5.0 million	0%
$ 5 million to $ 12.5 million	35%
$ 12.5 million to $ 50 million	45%
$ 50 million to $ 150 million	55%
Above $ 150 million	65%

Note that, as the rationale is based on income, the brackets refer to the inheritance received by each heir. Regarding the tax rates, just like income taxes, the taxation of inheritance has to be progressive.

Finally, as inheritance is a transfer of wealth, all the obstacles and the approaches to get over them discussed above for Extreme-Wealth Taxes are also valid for extreme-inheritance taxes.

CHAPTER 6

ALTERNATE PATHS
ALTERNATE ENDS

6.1   The Middle Class And The Western Social Order

An Advanced Definition Of The Middle Class

Within the framework of the Fundamental Awareness series, the definition of the middle class needs to be advanced beyond its common definition based on income alone, to enable the proper analysis of its vitality for the western social order.

The advanced definition of a *real middle class* needs to be based on *two vital attributes that must exist simultaneously.*

First, *each member of the middle class should have an income level much above that of bare-survival, so that the middle class can develop a demand for social values like individual rights and freedoms, fairness, dignity, etc. beyond basic material needs.* From the society's perspective, this necessitates a minimum level of income per capita, provided that the total income of the society is distributed within -or at least close to- the boundaries of acceptable inequality.

And second, *each member of the middle class should have an intellectual level much above that of being intellectually-childish,* based on some (self-attained or -preferably- formal) social education and experience *that enables them to develop some social awareness on economic and political issues.* From the society's perspective, this necessitates a minimum average level of Social Intellect.

To reemphasize, *only a middle class that fits into this advanced definition will serve as the guardian and the stabiliser of the western social order.*

The rationale behind this argument will be explained in the rest of this section. First the natural emergence of a real middle class will be analysed. This analysis will reveal why this real middle class will not only protect the western social order but also support economic growth. Then, it will explain how and why this real middle class may weaken or even disappear in time with serious consequences for the social order of the society. And finally, how the real middle class can be protected to avoid facing the negative consequences of its disappearance.

How A Real Middle Class Emerges

As mentioned above, for the birth of a real middle class, both some threshold income level and some threshold intellectual level have to be passed by very many individuals in the society. And these two are not independent attributes, and in the natural flow, they will rather develop - and then exist- in a chicken-and-egg fashion. Consider a society that is weak in both economic and intellectual fronts to start with. Initially some expertise on some specific economic activity develops and generates value through merit and hard work, which in turn generates some additional income, which in turn gives the chance to the current generation to educate their next generation a little better, both professionally and socially, who in turn will create further economic value and further income, and consequently educate their children much better on both fronts, who in turn will earn even more income and so on. Through this repetitive process where each generation gets more wealthy and more intellectual than the previous one, a real middle class will eventually emerge and strengthen within the society, and at some point will start to demand social values, eventually including Free Markets and Democracy.

On the surface, this process looks rather simple and trivial, moreover, inevitable and unidirectional. But the devil is in the details, and nothing is as trivial as it looks.

It is crucial that *the process needs to be initially ignited and continuously fed by an increase in income obtained through utilizing merit by very many people within the society.* Any income obtained without merit, say through luck or excessive risk taking or cheating[49], neither requires nor promotes the development of either the professional or the intellectual capacity of the individuals, and therefore, even if the society accumulates wealth eventually, it does not ever create a demand for any social values, let alone competitive markets and Democracy. That is exactly why many developing societies with huge natural resources -existence of which is a matter of pure luck-, may attain tremendous wealth and even distribute some of this wealth to many of their citizens, but never develop a real middle class defined in the manner above, as such wealth does not promote either professional education or intellectual development.

To reemphasize, accumulated wealth alone does not demand, and therefore does not develop, either social values or Free Markets or Democracy, even if it may be distributed widely within the society. Only the chain reaction of professional work and following economic success based on it, coupled with social education and rising social awareness, does.

Why A Real Middle Class Supports Both The Stability Of The Social Order And The Economic Growth

For the sake of the simplicity of the following discussion, assume that the society is made up of three classes : an economic upper class (with or without adequate Social Intellect), a real middle class as defined above (with adequate income and adequate Social Intellect), and a lower economic class (with or without adequate Social Intellect).

Notice that the definition above is tricky: a society may have three *economic classes* (upper, middle and lower), but no real middle class in the way defined by the beginning of this section. In such a society the two major contributions of the real middle class discussed below will not exist at all. The discussion below assumes that there is a real middle class in the society.

THE STRONGER THE REAL MIDDLE CLASS THE MORE STABLE THE SOCIAL ORDER

From an economic perspective, as explained in Book Two of this series, those in the upper economic class commonly want to lock in, and preferably improve, their dominant status in the economy, through decreasing competition and further concentrating their economic powers, consequently rising inequality towards excessive levels at the expense of everybody else, including the middle class. Naturally, this will not be supported by the middle class, as it means too big a transfer of income and wealth out of the middle class to the upper class. Those in the lower economic class, on the contrary, want too much taxation-and-distribution to minimise the inequality harming them. And this will not be supported by the middle class either, as it means too big a transfer of income and wealth out of the middle class to the lower class. Moreover, as discussed in Section 1.2, although they are contrary in essence, both what the upper class wants (increasing inequality too much) and what the lower class wants (decreasing inequality too much), will consequently decrease the growth rate of the economy at the expense of everybody, including the middle class. It is primarily those in the middle class that demand both free and fair competition for higher economic growth to improve their material and social status, and just some optimal dose of taxation-and-distribution as a means of rational protection against the unescapable risks of life, keeping inequality at moderate levels.

From a political perspective, again as explained in Book Two, those in the upper economic class commonly want to keep their dominant status, through misguiding both the intellectually-childish and the politicians, or trying to buy out politicians and bureaucrats if possible, or even supporting or cooperating with concentrated political powers provided that their interests are protected in return. Those in the lower economic class, on the contrary, are ready to change or even destroy the social order, commonly falling prey to populist promises that are practically unrealizable in practice. It is primarily those in the middle class that demand the social values like human rights and freedoms, the rule of law, and the legitimacy and accountability of the state governance through Democracy, and support the continuation of the current western social order with only incremental changes to adapt to the necessities of changing times and conditions.

In short and simple terms, the upper class has too much to protect and thus prefer sustainable concentrations of power in both the economy and the political arena, deteriorating the western social order. The lower class has too little to lose and thus may prefer extreme redistribution destroying the economic system, or anarchy destroying the political system, either naively believing in some empty promises or to take revenge from the rest of the society in case they have no hope left. Therefore, *it is primarily those in the middle class that want the continuation of Free Market Economy and a well-functioning liberal Democracy, both to keep what they already have, and to have the freedom to further improve their material and social status.* Therefore, *the stronger the real middle class, the more they can promote and protect Free Markets and Democracy, and the more sustainable will be the western social order.*

THE STRONGER THE REAL MIDDLE CLASS THE HIGHER THE ECONOMIC GROWTH

As discussed in Section 2.2, when the average Social Intellect of the society rises, the society will neither tolerate inequality to rise as much as before during the over-dose stage of the Liberal Policy, nor tolerate the growth rate to fall as much as before during the over-dose stage of the Social Policy. Consequently, it will react earlier in both cases in demanding a policy change, which in turn will maximise the growth rate.

From this perspective, the existence of a real middle class with adequate Social Intellect prevents both the Liberal and the Social Policies to reach their extremes, with two significant consequences. First, this will decrease the risk of passing beyond Social Upheaval levels -as discussed in Section 2.1- and thus increase the stability of the western social order. And second, as explained in Section 2.2, this will increase the growth rate of the economy in the long run.

Therefore, *the stronger the real middle class, the higher will be the long-term growth rate of the economy.*

THE SIGNIFICANCE OF PRESERVING AND STRENGTHENING THE REAL MIDDLE CLASS

As the real middle class both supports the stability of the western social order and increases the growth rate of the economy in the long run, it becomes self-evident that each society needs to preserve and further strengthen its real middle class. However, the trends in almost all western societies during the last decades are just the opposite.

Therefore, a brief reminder of how the real middle class weakens is necessary.

How The Middle Class Weakens

Notice that the analysis of the emergence of a real middle class by the beginning of this section assumes that *very many people within the society* utilise their professional merit to increase their income in time, and consequently better educate their next generation both professionally and socially. From the viewpoint of the society, therefore, better professional and social education on a widespread basis for the next generation can be attained if and only if the society both passes beyond a certain income level and distributes that income to the current generation within an acceptable inequality level.

And this observation reveals an unfortunate reality: the process of developing and strengthening a real middle class is neither unstoppable nor irreversible, as the logic of the process described by the beginning of this section can easily run backwards – and at a much faster speed.

To illustrate how a real middle class can weaken so much so fast, assume that the society is initially at an optimal inequality level, where the inequality span, namely the difference between the individuals with the lowest incomes and those with the highest incomes, is neither too narrow nor too wide, but just within acceptable levels - as discussed in section 2.2. There is a strong real middle class that contains most of the population – just like it happens when the society approaches its Optimal Policy by the end of its current learning curve, again as discussed in Section 2.2. Naturally, the Social Intellect of the society, and thus of its middle class, is close to intellectually-adult level at this point in time. The optimal economic inequality in the society can then be represented by the inequality distribution at the middle of the vertical axis on Figure 1.1.B at Section 1.1, presented below as Figure 6.1.A. This is a very stable society, with a sustainable social order.

[6.1.A] OPTIMAL INEQUALITY

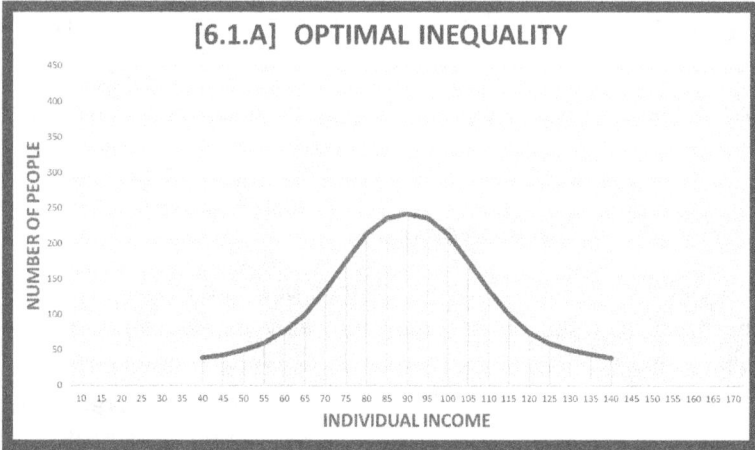

Then comes a set of major game changers one after the other within a short period of time, as it actually happened during the latest decades. The arrival of these game changers initially decreases the average Social Intellect of the society, and as the society falls back to the beginning of a new learning curve, there will be a shake up in most of the markets. New winners may arise in some markets, while existing winners may strengthen their position in some others. In both cases, the winners of the new economic environment will now have a chance to concentrate their economic power in their respective markets and to decrease competition, against the interest of the society -as discussed in detail in Book Two of this series- , as the Social Intellect of the society has not recovered yet. But such a fall in competition will immediately increase economic inequality, weakening the economic status of the middle class as well.

When economic inequality rises, the ones on the winning side of the inequality save more and thus lend more, while those on the losing side of the inequality borrow more for their consumption needs. Thus, a rise in economic inequality rises indebtedness among individuals, and with that, the stock of debt within a society rises – as have been happening in many societies during the last couple of decades. To make matters worse, the interest to be paid on the debt corresponds to a transfer of wealth from the borrowers to the lenders, further rising inequality. Thus, the cycle of inequality-rising-indebtedness-which-in-turn-is-rising-inequality-further feeds on itself[50].

As economic inequality continues to rise, the attention of the current middle class will be distracted to matters of survival, and consequently their social awareness will decrease further, as the world around is getting ever more complex every passing day while they have no time and effort left to cope up with the developments. This will mean a rise in intellectual inequality, which in turn enables the deliberate distraction of attention of many in the middle class to non-economic issues within politics or even away from politics, resulting in the failure of the check-and-balance relation between the economy and Democracy – as discussed in Chapter 3. Consequently, this will prevent or at least delay the political reaction necessary to shift towards more socially oriented policies, and economic inequality will rise further. And the society faces a spiral that feeds on itself on both the economic and the intellectual fronts.

To make matters worse, for the long run, the weakening of the income of the once-middle-class will prevent the proper professional and social education, and thus the intellectual development, of their coming generations. Consequently, the middle class weakens further and loses its dominance in the society.

Eventually, the society ends up with excessive inequality, on both the economic and intellectual fronts, as shown in Figure 6.1.B.

From the economic perspective, the population gets concentrated at the two extreme income levels, and the inequality span widens beyond acceptable and bearable limits. And now that there is no real middle class left to demand free and fair competition and liberal Democracy, from the political perspective, the social order is now totally unstable, sleeping on a time bomb of political upheaval.

[6.1.B] EXCESSIVE INEQUALITY

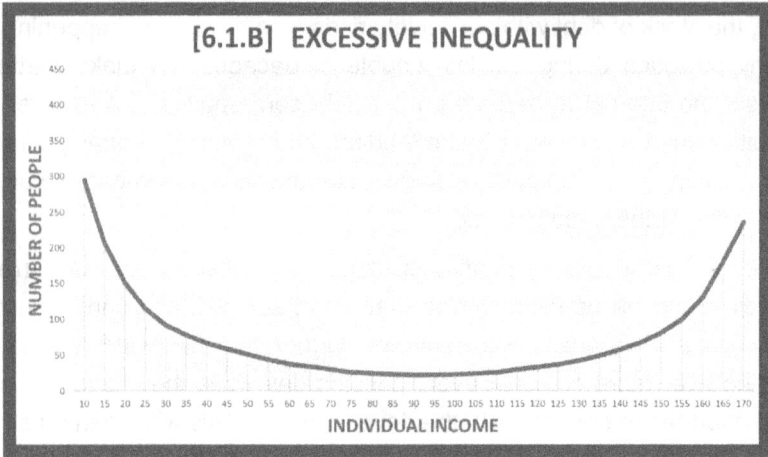

Therefore, the protection of the middle class, to avoid facing the catastrophic consequences of its disappearance, is of utmost importance for the future of the society. And it can only be done if the necessary structures are established *before* major game changers arrive.

Protecting The Real Middle Class

Within the jargon of Section 2.3, each time a game changer hits, Social Intellect may weaken and economic inequality may rise.

If the game changer is of limited strength, the loss of Social Intellect and the rise in economic inequality will be marginal, and recovery will be faster and easier.

Unfortunately, sometimes the game changer is so strong that, Social Intellect falls too much, Fair Competition weakens or even ceases to exist, many extreme-winners and extreme-losers emerge, economic inequality rises too much, and the middle class weakens economically and intellectually. And this time, the path for the recovery of Social Intellect and the re-strengthening of the real middle class will take much longer, during which the stability of the social order may fall in danger. Therefore, *the society needs to ensure that its social order will survive during the time required for the recovery of Social Intellect and the re-strengthening of its real middle class.*

To protect its social order, the society needs to have a *previously established* taxation-and-distribution system that will stay functional throughout the recovery period. A social security system designed in line with the principles outlined in Chapters 4 and 5, will ensure that during the time required for the recovery, the taxation of the extreme-winners will finance the extreme-losers who are in-need, and consequently, any potential social reaction by the extreme-losers that may endanger the stability of the social order will be prevented.

Notice that, when a major game changer hits, and Fair Competition weakens or disappears, the taxation-and-distribution system temporarily takes the centre stage and keeps economic inequality within boundaries to ensure the stability of the social order. But for this to happen, the taxation-and-distribution system has to be pre-structured and fully functional when the major game changer hits, so that it can provide enough time for the recovery of the Social Intellect and Fair Competition, and the re-strengthening of the middle class. During this temporary period, the volume of taxation-and-distribution will be much higher than usual, as there will be more extreme-losers and extreme-winners.

Once Social Intellect recovers, Fair Competition is reestablished up to some extent, inequality falls back from excessive levels, and the middle class re-strengthens, the volume of required taxation-and-distribution decreases (in line with the decrease in the number of extreme-winners and extreme-losers), and the social order stabilizes naturally. Then, once again, taxation-and-distribution will become the supportive system behind Fair Competition in optimising inequality.

In short, *at times of temporary chaos following the arrival of a major game changer, the taxation-and-distribution system is the insurance policy of the social order, keeping economic inequality within boundaries and preventing it from endangering the stability of the social order.*

That being said, it is important to reemphasize that, *heavy taxation-and-distribution can only be sustainable in the short to medium run*, while it supports the stability of the social order and provides adequate time for

Social Intellect to recover and restrengthen the real middle class through reestablishing Fair Competition. In the long run, however, it is impossible to sustain heavy taxation-and-distribution if pre-tax inequality remains high due to lack of Fair Competition, as explained in Chapter 4. *The only solution for the optimisation of inequality and the preservation of the real middle class in the long run is developing adequate Social Intellect and establishing Fair Competition.*

Needless to say, if Social Intellect can not recover and Fair Competition can not be established in the long run, the heavy taxation-and-distribution system will eventually collapse, taking the social order with itself into chaos. For that reason, recovering Social Intellect as fast as possible - through the means discussed in Book One- is the key for the sustainability of the social order.

6.2 Alternate Paths

Optimising Economic Inequality And Maximising Welfare, Recap

Chapters 1 and 2 explained the need for the existence of economic inequality, provided that it is optimised around moderate levels through establishing Fair Competition in the economy. Chapters 4 and 5 took this optimisation further through taxation-and-distribution, by enforcing boundaries at the bottom (through social security measures) and at the top (through taxes on extreme-success). Combining these concepts with the discussions of Social Intellect in Book One and Fair Competition in Book Two, reveals that,

- rising the Social Intellect of the society to adequate levels
- establishing Fair Competition as the primary optimiser of inequality
- establishing an optimal social security system
- establishing an optimal taxation system for extreme-success

will together enable approaching optimal inequality, and consequently approaching optimal growth rate and maximising welfare in the long run.

These being said, it is important to remind and reemphasize a few facts from the previous books in the series.

As discussed in Book One, Social Intellect is a blend of social education, experience and awareness. It is a relative concept, in the sense that, what really matters in practise is the intellectual level of the society compared to the complexity of the economic and political environment in which it needs to survive. If the pace of change in the complexity of the economic, political and social environment speeds up beyond the pace of rise in the Social Intellect of the society, the society loses its ability to understand the economic and political environment, and becomes open to be manipulated to make choices that transfer economic and political power to concentrated interest groups who serve their own interests at the expense of the society. And then, Free Market Economy and Democracy start to fail to serve their functions.

It directly follows that, *in today's economic, political and social environment, where technology develops and global integration continues at breakneck speeds,* unless deliberately kept at adequate levels through social education and other means discussed in Book One (like establishing independent sources of information and analysis, etc.), *Social Intellect has a natural tendency to fall.*

As discussed in Book Two, Fair Competition is a product of Social Intellect. In addition to free competition where success should stem from merit, and not through luck or cheating, Fair Competition encompasses fair opportunity for education and employment, and the necessary regulatory structures to protect and promote the interests of the society. The trouble with establishing and sustaining Fair Competition is that, unless it is ensured that nobody can cheat, everybody will have to start to cheat sooner or later. And ensuring the fair play of all competitors requires sustaining of a high level of Social Intellect.

Unfortunately, as Social Intellect has a natural tendency to fall in today's environment, it follows that, cheating has a natural tendency to spread, and consequently create concentrations of power in both economics and politics, which eventually harm the interests of the society.

These basic concepts in Books One and Two, can now be integrated with the discussions in the previous chapters of this book, to reveal two potential outcomes for the long run for a society: one when the society succeeds in realizing the conditions above, and the other when the society fails.

The Bright Scenario

In the Bright Scenario all the conditions for optimising inequality and economic growth are fulfilled at least satisfactorily, if not perfectly. As a result the welfare of the society will be maximised in the long run, while the stability of the social order of the society will be preserved.

To wrap up, in the Bright Scenario:

- The Social Intellect of the society reaches to adequate levels and stays there, through social education and continuously rising social awareness in line with economical, political, social and technological developments.

- As a direct result of attaining adequate Social Intellect, the attention of the society will not (and can not) be distracted away from politics and from economic issues within politics – as discussed in Chapter 3.
- Fair Competition will dominate economics and politics, and cheating in both will be minimised.
- Concentrations of power in economics, and consequently decreases in competition in various markets, will be prevented in the economy.
- An optimal structure of taxation-and-distribution will be established, to enable the fine tuning of inequality within the society at times when Fair Competition may not be adequate, and to prevent any concentrated economic power from casting a shadow on politics.
- Recovery will be fast even after major game changers, as the taxation-and-distribution system will function as a temporary insurance, and consequently, stability of the social order is preserved, increases in intellectual and economic inequalities can be kept within boundaries, and the middle class never weakens too much.
- Concentration of power will be prevented in politics, as a result of both the adequate social awareness of the society, and the prevention of concentrations of power in economics that may support or cooperate with political agents.
- And finally, the democratic system can be re-structured to better serve the needs of the society in today's environment, as will be discussed in Book Four of this series.

The Dark Scenario

The Dark Scenario, which was never explicitly mentioned before in this series, is the natural opposite of the Bright Scenario. It emerges when none of the conditions for optimising inequality and economic growth are fulfilled.

Consequently,

- The Social Intellect of the society will persistently stay below adequate levels, due to the lack of social education and continuously falling social awareness against the economical, political, social and technological developments.
- This will give rise to extreme intellectual inequality within the society, where those with social awareness -with good or bad intentions- will just be a minority, and there will be a huge gap between their Social Intellect and that of the majority of the society.
- As a direct result of inadequate Social Intellect, the attention of the society will and can be easily distracted away from politics and from economic issues within politics, making them easy targets for manipulation towards serving the interests of others rather than their own.
- Fair Competition will weaken and eventually disappear, and cheating will dominate economics and politics.
- Concentrations of power in economics will rise, and consequently there will be under-competition in some markets, and over-competition in others, both harmful for the welfare of the society – as discussed in Book Two.
- A functional taxation-and-distribution structure can not be established, as concentrated powers in economics will utilise their political influence to resist to be taxed as necessary.
- Recovery will be very slow after major game changers, as increases in economic and intellectual inequalities weaken the middle class for a long time or even permanently. Inequality, growth and welfare will get worse after each game changer as the majority of the society irrevocably loses their Social Intellect.

- As a result of all these, economic inequality will eventually rise to excessive levels, economic growth will severely decrease from its full potential, and welfare of the society will be minimised.
- Stability of the social order will then be severely endangered.
- Some concentration of power may and probably will emerge in politics, with the support or cooperation of the concentrated economic powers, that will not be representing the interests of the society anymore. Even if the social order and the cover of Democracy may be sustained somehow, the economic and political systems will cease to serve the society.
- Eventually, an economically and intellectually superior minority will dominate and run both the economy and the political system, while the intellectually-childish majority will be living in marginal economic conditions, such that their attention is primarily focused on economic survival and/or distracted away from politics and economic issues in politics - as described in Chapter 3.

The Trouble With The Natural Tendency

It is tempting to think that in practise most societies will end up somewhere in between the Bright and the Dark scenarios in the long run. Unfortunately, that may not be the case.

Although the two basic scenarios above represent the two extreme cases, they share a common characteristic: once attained, they are sustainable. On the contrary, any scenario in between will probably be unsustainable, and will drift towards one of these basic scenarios in time[51].

And the even more unfortunate fact is that, unless a society with a high level of Social Intellect deliberately choses to reach the Bright Scenario and carefully preserves it, *under today's conditions, the economic and political systems will naturally drift towards the Dark Scenario.*

The Carrot And The Stick, Again

The crucial question, therefore, is how the fundamental awareness of the society can be enhanced to enable the society to deliberately take the path towards the Bright Scenario, rather than naturally falling into the Dark Scenario.

As there is no place for heroes in a Democracy -as discussed in Book One-, unless the society realizes that it has to increase its Social Intellect and awareness to adequate levels to be able to move towards the Bright Scenario and escape the dark one, no one can save the society from its inevitable destiny.

Therefore, how can the society be persuaded to try hard to increase its Social Intellect?

One approach can be promoting the Bright Scenario. That is equivalent to presenting a carrot within the jargon of Section 4.4. It primarily calls for a turn to rationality, creating positive expectations within a scientific framework.

Another approach can be explaining and warning against the Dark Scenario. That is equivalent to creating a stick within the jargon of Section 4.4. Although this may still seem to be a call for rationality, through creating negative expectations this time by showing the other side of the same coin, in practise it creates a further emotional dimension based on the fear of the Dark Scenario.

And *in societies with inadequate Social Intellect, the heart dominates the brain, and the stick dominates the carrot, and thus the fear of the dark will be much more motivating than the promise of the sunshine.*

To illustrate again, consider a case where a man in his 50's, who smoke heavily, is visiting a doctor. One doctor shows him the carrot and says that if he quits smoking he will add 10 years to his lifespan – some benefit in some distant future. The other doctor shows him the stick and says if he does not quit smoking he will die within 5 years – a clear and present danger. Although what the two doctors say are the opposite sides of the same coin, it is not difficult to guess which one will be more effective in making him quit smoking.

Indeed, the case with the Bright and the Dark Scenarios is similar. The Bright Scenario will be realised in the long run, as the positive developments will come continuously but gradually. Thus, its benefit is in the distant future.

However, the Dark Scenario may proceed real fast, as Democracy -and consequently Free Market Economy- may collapse suddenly (or pass the point of no return) in a very near future, if negative trends reign. Thus, it is a clear and present danger.

Therefore, presenting the immediate danger of facing the Dark Scenario is not only necessary, but will also be more effective on changing the behaviour of the societies towards trying harder to rise their Social Intellect. And that is exactly why the dark side of the coin is presented together with the bright side in this section.

Needless to say, a third approach, which looks best in principle, can be utilising both the carrot and the stick simultaneously. In practise, however, considering the very limited attention span of the current societies, and the fact that the stick is a better motivator than the carrot, it makes more sense to fully concentrate on the stick and not to waste time with the carrot, in motivating the society to develop its Social Intellect and awareness to an adequate level.

And even if the stick succeeds to motivate the society, the path to developing Social Intellect and Fundamental Awareness on economic and political issues is neither easy nor guaranteed to end in success. However, there is no other way to escape from the Dark Scenario.

CONCLUSION

MAXIMUM GROWTH RATE IS ACHIEVED AT MODERATE INEQUALITY LEVELS

When inequality moves away from moderate levels, and either rises too much or falls too much towards extreme levels, the growth rate falls. Similarly, when inequality is moving from either of the extremes towards moderate levels, the growth rate rises. Maximum growth rate is achieved around moderate inequality levels.

WELFARE DEPENDS ON BOTH ECONOMIC GROWTH AND INEQUALITY

The welfare of the society depends on both the economic growth rate and the level of inequality within the society, through a non-linear and interdependent relation, such that welfare falls to minimum levels either when inequality is too high or when growth rate is too low. To maximise its welfare, a society needs to balance its growth rate and inequality, staying away from either a too low growth rate or a too high inequality.

RISING SOCIAL INTELLECT AND ESTABLISHING FAIR COMPETITION INCREASES WELFARE

The higher the Social Intellect of a society, the lower its tolerance for too much of a rise in inequality or too much of a fall in growth rate, or simply, for too much of a fall in welfare. This in practise moderates the policy cycles, and results in higher average growth rates and lower average inequality levels, increasing welfare in the long run.

And more important than that, as Social Intellect rises, Fair Competition is better established, which in turn enables much higher growth rates at any level of inequality, and ensures a further major rise in the welfare.

THE SOCIETY TRAVELS ON A LEARNING CURVE TO MAXIMISE ITS WELFARE

The gradual improvements from one policy cycle to the next, due to rising Social Intellect through gathering experience, corresponds to travelling on a learning curve, better optimising inequality and economic growth, and consequently increasing welfare by each cycle.

MAJOR GAME CHANGERS RESULT IN A FALL IN SOCIAL INTELLECT AND NECESSITATE TO START A NEW TRAVEL ON A NEW LEARNING CURVE

At times some very major developments, like the technological advancements and the fast spread of globalisation in the recent decades, which can be called game changers, significantly rise the complexity of the economic and political environment within a relatively short time, consequently weakening the Social Intellect of the society and necessitating a new travel on a new learning curve in search for new optimal inequality and economic growth levels.

SOCIAL SECURITY IS THE SUPPORTER AND THE STABILIZER

The society should primarily establish Fair Competition to sustain inequality around moderate levels, and further support the system with optimised social security to take care of any residual or temporary fluctuations.

And at times of major changes when Fair Competition is heavily diluted and requires a longer than usual recovery time during which the social order needs to be sustained, social security will preserve the stability of the economic and political systems.

TAXATION OF EXTREME-SUCCESS IS FAIR AND NECESSARY

Extreme-success is based on either natural or self-fabricated extreme-good-luck, and therefore is not fair, making its further taxation fair. And such taxation is necessary, as extreme-success results in a concentration of economic power, which not only causes a misallocation of resources, but also seeks political influence to protect its interests against those of the society.

Although the lack of cooperation between societies seems to be a major obstacle against such taxes, in case the western societies can cooperate among themselves, the flow of funds (to escape taxation) towards societies with unreliable rule of law will remain marginal, and the taxation of extreme-success will work.

WHEN SOCIAL INTELLECT WEAKENS DEMOCRACY FAILS TO FUNCTION

When the Social Intellect of the society weakens for any reason, the attention of the society can easily be distracted to non-economic issues in politics, or worse, totally away from politics. Once that happens, Democracy starts to fail to cure too high inequality or any other economic troubles, as the check-and-balance relation between economics and politics disappears in practise. Then, concentrated interests will dominate economics and politics, cooperating with each other and promoting their own agendas at the expense of the society.

THE SOCIETY NATURALLY DRIFTS TOWARDS THE DARK SCENARIO, UNLESS DELIBERATELY CHOOSES TO GO FOR THE BRIGHT ONE THROUGH RISING AND SUSTAINING ITS SOCIAL AWARENESS

Social Intellect has a natural tendency to fall, as a society either does not try hard enough to keep its social awareness, or fails to do so against the frequent arrival of major game changers, or both. Consequently, cheating spreads and creates concentrations of power in both economics and politics, and the society naturally drifts towards the Dark Scenario.

The call to wake up a society has to focus on presenting the immediate danger of facing the Dark Scenario and persuading the society to try harder to rise its Social Intellect and awareness, before the deterioration of its social order passes the point of no return.

BOOK FOUR OF THE SERIES

Wishfully assuming that the society will choose to move towards the Bright Scenario, the next vital step will be implementing the necessary structural enhancements in its political system – as will be discussed in Book Four, which will tie ends with Books One, Two and Three, to complete the political part of the overall puzzle.

THE AUTHOR

Salih Reisoglu has served as the CEO of an Investment Management Company for 20 years, and is an expert on Capital Markets with over 35 years of experience in analysing economics and politics. He is a regular guest speaker on many TV channels and universities. He holds an MSc in Computer Engineering from Lehigh University, and an MBA in Finance from The Wharton School of the University of Pennsylvania.

INDEX OF KEY CONCEPTS

ENDNOTES

---

[1] COMPOUNDING EFFECTS IN THE LONG RUN

As mentioned in the main text, growth rates do *not* add up, but are compounded. Assume that the annual growth rates of an economy for each year within a long term of n years are ST1, ST2, ... STn, and its overall growth rate for the whole term of n years is LT.

If one tries to approximate LT through adding up annual rates, one mistakenly calculates

LT = ST1 + ST2 + ... + STn

However, in fact, through compounding,

(1+LT) = (1+ST1) * (1+ST2)* ..... (1+STn)

For small values of ST, which is mostly the case in practise, the two equations above give similar results for the short term (say for 3 periods). But for the long term, their difference is huge, and thus adding up can *not* be used as an approximation for the real case – namely compounding.

For instance, assume ST growth rate is constant at 4% throughout the years.

For 3 years,

first formula (approximation) gives LT = 4% + 4% + 4% = 12%,

while in reality LT = [1.04*1.04*1.04] – 1 = 12.5%.

But for 30 years,

first formula (approximation) gives LT = (4% + 4% + ... 4%) = 30 * 4% = 120%,

while in reality LT = [1.04*1.04*....1.04] – 1 = [(1.04)^30] – 1 = 224%.

---

[2] Or, with outdated regulation failing to provide and protect Fair Competition.

[3] A CLOSER LOOK AT THE FINANCING OF CONSUMPTION WITH CREDITS

The credit system, where those with excess funds place their savings in the financial system so that those in need of funds can borrow them, is at the core of the economic system of the western societies, and fuels the economic growth when used in the right manner. Credits can even out an individual's consumption or a company's spending throughout time, as credit is meant to be received when revenues are limited and expected to be paid back when revenues and cash flows increase. This way, credits enable the management of the timing of short-term expenses versus long-term revenues. Alternatively, credits can finance an individual's or company's investments, to be paid back when those investments bear fruit. In this way they enable investments at every scale, which is a crucial need for the long-term economic growth of the society. In short, credits are valuable and supportive of the society's welfare, *provided that they are eventually paid back.* In other words, credits are beneficial to the society when they are given *by the current winners of the system, to the winners of the future.*

On the contrary, *when credits are given to the current losers of the system who will continue to stay to be losers in the future, they serve no purpose but to collapse the system in the long run.* That is because the right way to help the losers in the system is not through supplying credits, but through taxation and redistribution, namely through applying appropriate Social Policies, as will be discussed in the coming chapters. However, when credits are extended to the potential losers of the system, they just enable the losers to sustain their spending in the short run and prevent them from realizing that their financial situation is actually deteriorating, which in turn delays their political reaction to demand more socially oriented policies – as will be discussed in the coming chapters.

In other words, when there are irrational increases in the amount of credit in the financial system, the losers' consumption relative to that of the society may not reflect the change in their income relative to the change of the income of the society. This is exactly what has happened during the years before the 2008 crisis, during which the booming credits in the system (in the US, EU and elsewhere), decreased the consumption (and the Housing Investment) gap between the losers and the winners, hiding the fact that the income gap is actually increasing. And eventually came the crisis.

As the society has to live with the credit system, the solution simply lies with the proper regulation of the whole financial system, to make sure that credits are extended only to those who have the potential to pay them back in the future. And that is a political issue rather than an economic one.

[4] To make matters worse, such a rise in demand failing to face a counter rise in supply, will just cause an increase in prices, namely inflation. That will make the situation even more unbearable for the low-income earners.

[5] This is why many empirical studies find contradicting results or come out to be inconclusive: they mistakenly focus *solely on the direction of change in inequality* which naturally gives different results at different stages.

[6] And vice versa: The absolute incomes of individuals fall if the economic growth rate is negative, and the speed of the fall of absolute incomes increase as growth rate falls to further negative values.

[7] Under the assumption of no growth, when inequality increases, those on the losing side of the rising inequality will practically lose both their relative income and absolute income. Similarly, those on the winning side of the rising inequality will practically increase both their relative income and absolute income.

[8] And vice versa: In practise, if an individual is on the losing side of the inequality (i.e. his personal income is below the average income of the society) to start with, then most probably he will benefit from decreasing inequality. But if an individual is on the winning side of the inequality (i.e. his personal income is above the average income of the society) to start with, then he will most probably lose some of his benefits under decreasing inequality.

[9] In mathematical terms, the society has a total income of (10*$20 + 10*$40 + 10*$80 =) $1400. The average income is ($1400 / 30 people =) $46.7. These reamin the same after all distribution cases. In the initial case, the range of inequality is $60 (between $20 and $80), and the lowest earning people are $26.7 below average while the highest earning people are $33.3 above average. After the distribution in the first case, the range of inequality rises to $80 (between $15 and $95), the lowest earning people now earn $15 which is $31.7 below average, and the highest earning person now earns $95 which is $48.3 above average. Thus, both the absolute and the relative incomes of the losers decrease (in turn, decreasing their Welfare), while both the absolute and the relative incomes of the winner increase (in turn, increasing his Welfare).

[10] In the mathematical jargon, the relation of Welfare with these two variables is both non-linear and interdependent, practically meaning that the amount of change in Welfare resulting from a unit change in one of the variables, will depend on both of the variables' prevailing levels.

[11] When maximum Welfare is reached at an economic growth level that is below the maximum growth level, it is rational to expect that the society will prefer to have a lower inequality to trade for a lower-than-maximum-growth. Thus, the projection of the maximum Welfare point on the grey plane will be on the lower inequality side of the maximum growth point.

[12] Please refer to Book Two of this series, *Competition and Cheating*, for the detailed discussion of all these issues.

[13] Even if rising inequality does not decrease economic growth too much, it still decreases the Welfare of the society, as its effect will be dominant at high inequality levels. Thus, a change from Liberal to Social Policy will still be demanded by the society at the high inequality threshold level. The exact relation of inequality with economic growth does not change this conclusion.

[14] In practise, individuals can not know the changes in their own income relative to the changes in the income of the others in the society, but can only observe the changes in their own consumption relative to the changes in the consumption of others in the society, in their efforts to judge whether inequality is changing for or against their benefit. Consider the case of rising income inequality within a society during the over-dose stage of the Liberal Policy. As individuals can not easily observe the changes in income inequality, but just observe the changes in consumption inequality, they need to make the assumption that, any changes in income inequality will be directly reflected to, and hence can be detected through, the changes in consumption inequality. However, while income inequality is rising on the one hand, if the financial system can increase the credit supply significantly and feed the people with fresh credit on the other hand, their consumption will rise out of line with their income. Their observation will naturally be that consumption inequality is falling and hence income inequality must be falling too, while, actually income inequality is rising and is going unobserved. Thus, there will not be a political reaction, namely any demand for a policy reversal in the short run. Sooner or later, the society faces the bitter reality that decreasing consumption inequality is based on the spread of credits in the financial system, and not on decreasing income inequality, and therefore, it is simply not sustainable. At the moment of this sudden realisation, which usually comes with an economic crisis, the actual income inequality might have already passed beyond the *high inequality*

system breakdown level. Then, a strong political reaction will emerge, and unless an immediate political reply (like an early election resulting in a change of policy) comes, the social order of the society may fall in danger.

[15] Notice that, as shown in Figure 2.1.B, the growth rate when Welfare reaches its minimum level at the reversal point from Social to Liberal Policy (PC_{LBR}), is assumed to be lower than the growth rate when Welfare reaches its minimum level at the reversal point from Liberal to Social Policy (PC_{SCL}). The reason behind this assumption is that, when inequality is very low (as in the end of the over-dose stage of Social Policy) the society can bear worse levels of economic growth rate before giving a political reaction. Or, reading backwards, the society can not stand too high inequality (as in the over-dose stage of Liberal Policy) even if economic growth rate is way above the case where inequality is low. For that reason, the minimum level of growth rate is expected to occur at the reversal point from Social to Liberal Policy (PC_{LBR}).

[16] When the Social Intellect of the society is low, the low growth rate threshold may actually be at negative levels, i.e. the economy may actually shrink for some time before a demand for a policy change (from social to liberal) emerges and the actual change occurs. As the Social Intellect of the society rises, the low growth rate threshold will rise to low positive growth rates, i.e. at least the economy will continue to grow - albeit slowly- until the policy change occurs.

[17] Even when the producers and consumers meet under conditions of free and perfect competition, and are both happy with the formation of the market price, the outcome may still not be beneficial for the society at large. This happens when the transaction they agree to execute may have consequences that effect some third parties within the society who are not on either side of the transaction. This creates a problem when these third parties are effected in a negative manner, practically meaning that they are unwillingly incurring a cost because of that transaction,

called an *externality* in the jargon, which actually should have been paid by one or both of the sides taking part in the transaction. Therefore, it is the duty of the regulator, as an agent of the society, to detect and prevent the emergence of such externalities, and in cases where they are inevitable, at least make sure through proper regulation that the sides to the relevant transaction carry the full costs of these externalities, rather than the society.

[18] As explained in Book Two, the term *well-regulated* corresponds to optimal regulation – not too little and not too much.

[19] Notice that, in simple terms, when cheating spreads, the slice of the cake the Cheaters get for themselves increase in size, while the total size of the cake shrinks, thus the slice of the cake the rest of the society gets shrinks faster than the cake itself. Therefore, *because of the fact that the overall economy is hurt by the mis-allocation of resources resulting from cheating, the harm the Cheaters inflict on the rest of the society is more than the benefit they extract for themselves.* It directly follows that, as cheating spreads, the inequality within the society (to the benefit of the Cheaters) rises sharply, and decreases the overall Welfare of the society.

[20] The process of policies learning from each other happens frequently in practise. One example from the recent past is the adaptation of some aspects of the liberal free market policies of the Reagan and Thatcher periods, by the Social Policy oriented leaders Clinton and Blair, in the US and the UK. In spite of the fact that both of those neo-liberal policies applied by the right wing parties contained extremes that were far away from being optimal, when the succeeding left wing parties in both countries adopted some milder value-generating versions of their principles and modified their previous approaches, they have actually improved their own policies one step ahead for the better, getting closer to an Optimal Policy.

[21] Indeed, this is the reason why the economic growth rate at the high inequality threshold discussed in Section 2.1 (at PC_{SCL} on Figure 2.1.B) is assumed to be way above that at the low growth rate threshold (GR_{MIN} at PC_{LBR}). At the low growth rate threshold, the average growth rate of the society is very low but at least the inequality between the members of the society is also very low – meaning that the burden of low growth is more or less equally shared. But when inequality is high, even at higher average growth rates for the society, a significant share of the population, namely those on the losing side of the inequality, actually experience a growth rate below the low growth threshold. Consequently, the political reaction comes earlier, at a higher average growth rate for the society.

[22] As discussed in Book One of this series, *causation* refers to the chain of events from the reason(s) to a particular result. Understanding the causation relation, therefore, refers to analysing and recognising the causes behind a certain outcome. In a world that becomes ever more complex every passing day, understanding causations are becoming more and more of a challenge for each society.

[23] It is important to emphasize that, in some cases, the politician sincerely believes the significance of the non-economic issue. He may be right or wrong, but at least he is not cheating. Thus, what he is doing is not deliberately distracting attention to irrelevant non-economic issues for his own benefit, but just trying to focus the society's attention on an issue that he believes to be significant. And, as will be discussed later in this section, on some occasions the non-economic issue may really be significant, and thus the politician may be right in his efforts in trying to focus the society's attention to that issue.

[24] Actually, what has happened in 2008 was not a "crisis" but an "outburst of accumulated structural damages" - as explained in Book One of this series.

[25] Just like what happens with the rest of the society, a major rise in the complexity of the environment will also push some Cheaters to the losers side while some new Cheaters will emerge on the winning side of the new income inequality. This is simply because even cheating requires new approaches to benefit from the new complex environment, which in turn requires the preservation of some more intellect with respect to the others – and thus some previously successful Cheaters will fail while new ones emerge.

[26] Needless to say, as discussed in Book One, not all the intellectually-adults are Cheaters, and some may try to cure the trouble through waking up the intellectually-children to reality. However, their chances of success will be minimal in practise, as explained in Section 3.3.

[27] As discussed in Book Two Section 3.2, in simple terms, the concept of *Comparative Advantage* states that each individual should do what he can do best relative to the others. For instance, he may produce $10 worth of some product A, and $20 worth of some product B within an hour. In absolute terms, he creates more value with product B within an hour, and thus may choose to do so when left to his own decision. However, others may be producing $2 worth of product A, and $50 worth of product B within an hour. In that society, it is best for the society if this individual produces A rather than B, as his comparative advantage over others is on A. (i.e. in this simple case, his productivity on A is much higher than others, while his productivity on B is much lower – making it better for the society when he produces A)

[28] The concept of being in-need and a similar approach will be presented while discussing the social security for the working-aged in the next section. However, it is crucial to emphasize a major difference between the working-aged and the elderly: contrary to the working-aged, there is no danger of loss of motivation for the elderly, as they are not in the labour force anyway, and therefore, a higher basic fixed-amount

compensation, if feasible from the viewpoint of economic sustainability, can be appropriate.

[29] Assume that the individual would accept to work for $1.000 without any direct compensation. Then, if a direct compensation amounting $250 is introduced, he will accept to work for $850, as now his total income will rise to $1.100 (=$850+$250). And now his employer will save $150. Therefore, $150 of the compensation subsidizes the employer, and only $100 will remain to be the net benefit of the individual.

[30] When the condition of need of financial support is considered, some operational details have to be fixed. For instance, the income and wealth of couples have to be considered in aggregate, albeit with somewhat higher minimal limits. And for families with children below the working-ages, these limits should naturally be higher.

[31] For a simple illustration, assume that there are two similar societies with similar social security structures. However, Society 1 has high inequality, while Society 2 has much lower inequality thanks to Fair Competition. In Society 1, the required size of taxation-and-distribution is 150 units, and the size of its overall economy (GNP) is 500 units. The burden of social security on the economy is therefore 150/500 = %30, which is most probably unsustainable. In Society 2, however, the establishment of Fair Competition has decreased pre-tax inequality such that the required size of taxation-and-distribution is 90 units, and has increased economic growth such that the size of its overall economy (GNP) is 600 units. The burden of social security on the economy is therefore 90/600 = %15, which is most probably sustainable. The main observation to be made here is that, small changes in inequality and economic growth, will result in a major change in the relative size of the required taxation-and-distribution with respect to the size of the economy, and will enable the social security system to be sustainable in the long run.

[32] FAIR COMPETITION AND TAXATION-AND-DISTRIBUTION: A CLOSER LOOK FROM THE VIEWPOINT OF ECONOMIC POLICIES DISCUSSED IN CHAPTER 2

As discussed in Chapter 2, the strength of social security (i.e. the dose of taxation-and-distribution) is a central theme in both the Social and Liberal Policies. The initial stages of each Social Policy starts with strengthening the social security, and the initial stages of each Liberal Policy starts with weakening it.

Regarding the Social Policy, when moderate inequality and high growth is achieved following the application of a stronger taxation-and-distribution system, usually during the maturity stage of some Social Policy discussed in Chapter 2, all may look so fine in the economy that, the society fails to decrease the strength of its social security system towards optimal levels. On the contrary, it may even strengthen it further, as the economy can now handle an even stronger social security system. Consequently, as the negative consequences of a too strong social security emerge later on (during the over-dose stage of Social Policy), economic growth starts to fall back towards the low-growth threshold, and eventually a policy change for the Liberal Policy is realised. And then social security is weakened again, and the cycle goes on as described in Chapter 2.

As long as the society fails to realise that once it establishes some conditions of Fair Competition, it needs to decrease the strength of its social security system accordingly, it will continue to oscillate on the same cycle of its learning curve, continuously strengthening and weakening its social security in the meantime. Only when the society realises that as Fair Competition is further established, the strength of the social security should be further decreased, it moves to the next cycle on its learning curve towards its Optimal Policy.

[33] The over-strengthening of social security until too high inequality falls to moderate levels can be rational. However, keeping it too strong after the initial purpose is served, mostly through borrowing in the short run, is irrational – as explained in the subsection above.

---

[34] Spending for the operations of the state cover all the vital institutions and operations of the state, so that the society will have a functioning economic and political system based on the rule of law, including Legislation, Execution, Jurisdiction and other vital governmental structures, plus domestic and international security, namely the police and the armed forces, and finally, all the social and economic infrastructure needed to support individual and corporate lives, like transportation, communications, utilities etc.

[35] In the economics jargon, printing money is expressed in terms of increases in the monetary base, which sounds much more professional. And actually, the simpler term used in this section, namely printing money, rarely refers to physical printing of any banknotes, but rather to increasing the money supply through extending credits and/or several other technical ways.

[36] Consumer price inflation is measured on a basket of goods and services, among which some may see price increases while others may experience price decreases, but what matters is the overall change in price of the basket. Similarly, asset price inflation can be measured on a basket of investment assets, from real estate to equities and bonds. Again some of these assets may experience price rises while others experience falls, but what matters is the overall change in price of the basket.

[37] When an individual buys investment assets, he does that with the aim to liquidate them in the future for further consumption. If the rise in the prices of these investment assets during their investment period comes out to be higher than the cumulative consumer price inflation during that period, the future purchasing power (i.e. consumption capability) of the individual will be higher than today in real terms. And vice versa.

[38] When people expect consumer price inflation to stay high in the future, they demand higher wages but do not resist increasing prices, both fuelling inflation further, which strengthens expectations further, creating a self-feeding cycle.

[39] Assume 1.073.741.824 players to be precise, a number chosen to be equal to 2^{30} for the simplicity of the illustration.

[40] The current brackets for income taxes and the corresponding tax rates, for most western societies, are similar to those at the table below.

INCOME BRACKETS (on Annual Income)	TAX RATES
0 – up to $ 50.000	10%
$ 50.000 to $ 100.000	20%-30%
$ 100.000 to $ 250.000	30%-40%
Above $ 250.000	35%-45%

At each bracket in the table, those in the United States resemble the lower rates and those in Western Europe resemble the higher rates.

[41] The first tax bracket usually resembles the income per capita in the society. As income/capita rises, the brackets may be revised up. The tax rates depend on how strong a state and how strong a social security system is desired. More strength requires higher tax rates in the long run.

[42] Further taxation, in principle, is introduced for taxing the excess returns of extreme-success that are obtained by the help of (natural or self-fabricated) extreme-good-luck. However, in practise, it is not easy to clearly define where common-high-success ends and extreme-success begins. Still, in most cases the extreme level is obvious without the need to define the fine line in between. And when a clear distinction has to be made in practise for tax purposes, it won't hurt to err to the benefit of

extreme-success. For instance, in the table with new brackets, the average annual income in the society is assumed to be around $50.000. In such a society, if someone earns say 20 times the average income per person in a society (i.e. up to $ 1 million), that can be accepted as common-high-success. But if he earns say 50 times or more (i.e. above $ 3 million), that can be considered as extreme-success.

[43] For a simple illustration assume that there are two individuals, A and B, such that their after-income-tax-revenues are $800 and $1500, respectively. Assume that they both spend $500 for their needs. If there is no consumption tax, A will save $300 and B will save $1000. The ratio of savings of A to savings of B, which will turn into the ratio of their wealth in the long run, will be 0.30. However, if there is consumption tax, of say 20% on spending, their will both spend $600 including consumption tax. Thus, A will save $200 and B will save $900. The ratio of savings of A to savings of B, which will turn into the ratio of their wealth in the long run, will then be 0.22. Therefore, *just because of the consumption tax*, the relative wealth of A with respect to B will be much lower, making A worse off, meaning that the gap between their wealth will be wider and thus *the wealth-inequality between them will be higher*.

[44] The multiplier 50 is just assumed to represent a rational level for extreme-success for this illustration. But in essence, it is just a round number coming out of thin air. Each society may decide on a different multiplier, based on its prevailing economic conditions and social norms.

[45] For instance, there are some applications and/or discussions on *regular wealth taxes* (starting from minor accumulations of wealth) in some societies, with very low tax rates (say 2%). In principle, this may serve to support the financing of the budget, but not to decrease political influence or improve allocation of resources. Therefore, in practise, such taxation is not worth its limited economic benefit with respect to the major fuss it creates in political terms.

[46] When the main purpose of Extreme-Wealth Taxes is set to be *to decrease the accumulated extreme-wealth in real terms* such it will not have any potential political influence, then the Extreme-Wealth Tax rate has to be above the real rate of return on the investment of the extreme-wealth.

In principle,

Real Rate of Return = [(1+Nominal Rate of Return) / (1+Inflation)] − 1

In low inflation economies like those of the western societies, this equation can be simplified to

Real Rate of Return = Nominal Rate of Return − Inflation

And the Nominal Rate of Return can be taken as some percentage points above the Risk Free Rate in the economy (namely the interest rate on the 10-year government bonds of the society).

A further variable that can be taken into account is the structure of the income taxes. In the current applications income taxes are generally applied on realised profits only, while most of the extreme-wealth owners utilise several financial structures to keep their profits "unrealised" even in the long run. Thus, under that circumstance, the Extreme-Wealth Tax rate for the initial threshold (i.e. the first bracket) can be defined as

Extreme-wealth tax rate at Threshold = Real Rate of Return + 5%

And under the current economic conditions in the US, this corresponds to a tax rate of approximately 10%, as used in the table.

Notice that at such a rate, the real decrease in wealth is actually around 5%, which practically means that, a fall towards the threshold wealth level, say from a level of (2 x Threshold) will take almost a quarter of a century. For that reason, any lower rates are meaningless. Actually, at any tax rate below the Real Rate of Return, the real value of wealth will continue to rise in spite of the wealth tax.

If someday income taxes are redesigned to take into consideration the unrealised profits, or the financial structures are somehow prevented to hide all capital gains (the unrealised income), then the formula above may include the income tax rate as another variable, such that,

Extreme-wealth tax rate at Threshold =

= [Nominal Rate of Return*(1 - Income Tax Rate)] – Inflation + 5%

Finally, if Inflation rises above single digit levels, both Extreme-Income Taxes and Extreme-Wealth Taxes should be reformulated to take inflation into account appropriately.

[47] THE EFFECTS OF EXTREME-WEALTH TAX

Assume that

Extreme-Wealth tax rate is t%,

Net (after Income-Tax) Real Return on Investment is r%,

then, after n years, what is left of the initial extreme-wealth above the threshold in real terms is approximately :

Residual wealth = (Initial wealth) * $(1- [t\% - r\%])^n$

For instance, if t=10%, r=6%, then, after 30 years,

Residual wealth = (Initial wealth)*$(1-[10\% - 6\%])^{30}$ = 0.29*(Initial wealth)

Therefore, contrary to common intuition, it will take 30 years for a tax rate of 10% to decrease the extreme-wealth to just below one-third of its initial value.

In another illustrative case, where the return on wealth is coming from a fast-growing business, say with r=10%, then even under the maximum tax rate of 20% for an extreme-wealth above the final bracket, after 20 years,

Residual wealth= (Initial wealth)*$(1-[20\% - 10\%])^{20}$ = 0.12*(Initial wealth)

Therefore, again contrary to common intuition, when the return on investment is high, it may take 20 years for a tax rate of even 20% to decrease the extreme-wealth towards the upper limit of the final bracket.

Finally, notice that, if r > t, then even after Extreme-Wealth Tax, wealth continues to increase in real terms.

[48] The economic crisis in 2008 necessitated some coordinated effort to prevent tax avoidance, and some major western societies started to cooperate better than before in recent years, through exchanging information and regulatory know-how. Although the cooperation issue is far from being solved on a global scale, at least the trend is in the right direction on both coasts of Atlantic.

[49] The different paths to success, namely merit, luck, excessive risk taking and cheating, are discussed in detail in Book Two of this series, *Competition and Cheating*.

[50] Notice that this vicious cycle arises when individuals have to borrow to consume. The case of borrowing to invest, where a rational investment will rise the revenue of the borrower in the future and will leave him a net benefit after paying back his debt and the interest on it, has nothing to do with this cycle. It is common that an individual borrows for both consumption and investment, and the outcome will then depend on which borrowing is dominant. If most of the accumulated debt was used for investment, the result may come out to be fine. However, if most of the accumulated debt was spent for consumption, trouble is on the horizon.

In principle, the financial sector primarily exists to bridge those who have the funds to lend with those who have the need to borrow to invest for their future, from financing their education to establishing new businesses. Unfortunately, in the latest decades the sector has diverted its attention to serving to those who need to borrow to consume (as a result of rising inequality), and that trend alone was, and still is, a significant sign of trouble - that the world had experienced during the 2008 crisis and will experience in the future again unless too high economic inequality is dealt with.

[51] Simply because of the fact that, Fair Competition is at the heart of the Bright Scenario, while lack of Fair Competition is at the heart of the Black Scenario. And as analysed in detail in Book Two, there are only two

possibilities regarding Fair Competition (versus cheating) in the long run: either nobody cheats, or everybody cheats. Any case in between is not sustainable, and will drift towards one of these two possibilities.

www.ingramcontent.com/pod-product-compliance
Lightning Source LLC
Chambersburg PA
CBHW050111280326
41933CB00010B/1059